URBAN TRAILS

VANCOUVER, BC

T0398120

URBAN
TRAILS
VANCOUVER, BC

**Surrey · Langley
Regional Parks · North Shore**

CRAIG ROMANO

MOUNTAINEERS
BOOKS

MOUNTAINEERS BOOKS is dedicated to the exploration, preservation, and enjoyment of outdoor and wilderness areas.

1001 SW Klickitat Way, Suite 201, Seattle, WA 98134
800-553-4453, www.mountaineersbooks.org

Printed in China
First edition, 2025

Design: Jen Grable
Layout: Cat Grishaver
Cartographer: Lohnes + Wright
All photographs by the author unless credited otherwise
Cover photograph: Sasamat Lake in təmtəmíxʷtən/Belcarra Regional Park (Trail 27)
Frontispiece: Downtown Vancouver from Queen Elizabeth Park (Trail 8)

Library of Congress Cataloging-in-Publication data is on file for this title at https://lccn.loc.gov/2024947363

Printed on FSC-certified materials.

ISBN (paperback): 978-1-68051-685-2
ISBN (ebook): 978-1-68051-686-9

An independent nonprofit publisher since 1960

CONTENTS

VANCOUVER

BURNABY & NEW WESTMINSTER

NORTH SHORE
BOWEN ISLAND

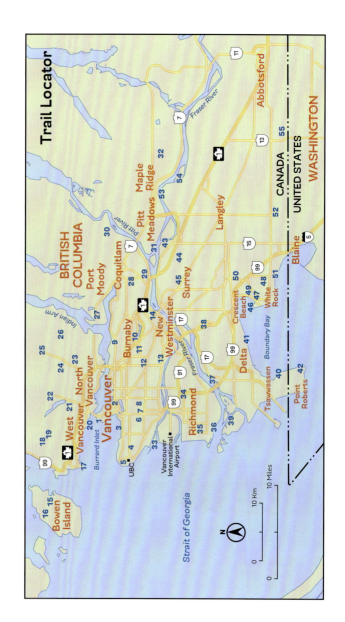

Trail Locator

TRAILS AT A GLANCE

Trail/Park	Distance	Walk	Hike	Run	Kids	Dogs	Bikes	Public Transit
VANCOUVER								
1. Stanley Park	More than 27 km (17 miles) of trails	•	•	•	•	•	•	•
2. Seawall	22.8 km (14.2 miles) one-way	•		•	•	•	•	•
3. Jericho, Locarno & Spanish Banks Beach Parks	4 km (2.5 miles) of beach; about 7.5 km (4.7 miles) of trails	•	•	•	•	•	•	•
4. Pacific Spirit Regional Park	More than 55 km (34 miles) of trails	•	•	•	•	•	•	•
5. Wreck Beach	More than 5 km (3 miles) of beach; about 2.5 km (1.5 miles) of trails	•	•		•	partial; restrictions		•
6. Arbutus Greenway	8.7 km (5.4 miles) one-way	•		•	•	•	•	•
7. VanDusen Botanical Garden	More than 7 km (4.3 miles) of trails	•			•			•
8. Queen Elizabeth Park	More than 5 km (3.1 miles) of trails	•		•	•	•		•
BURNABY & NEW WESTMINSTER								
9. Burnaby Mountain Conservation Area	More than 31 km (19 miles) of trails	•	•	•	•	•	•	•
10. Burnaby Lake Regional Park	More than 19 km (12 miles) of trails	•	•	•	•	•		•

Trail/Park	Distance	Walk	Hike	Run	Kids	Dogs	Bikes	Public Transit
11. Deer Lake	More than 12 km (7.5 miles) of trails	•	•	•	•	•		•
12. Central Park	More than 12 km (7.5 miles) of trails	•		•	•	•		•
13. Fraser Foreshore Trail	8 km (5 miles) one-way	•	•	•	•	•	•	•
14. Queen's and Glenbrook Ravine Parks	About 6 km (3.7 miles) of trails	•	•	•	•	•	•	•
NORTH SHORE								
15. Crippen Regional Park	11.4 km (7.1 miles) of trails	•	•	•	•	•		•
16. Mount Gardner	15.7 km (9.8 miles) roundtrip		•		•	•		•
17. Lighthouse Park	About 10 km (6.2 miles) of trails	•	•		•	•		•
18. Yew Lake & Black Mountain	2.3 km (1.4 mile) loop/9 km (5.6 miles) roundtrip	•	•		•	no Yew Lake		
19. Blue Gentian Lake & Hollyburn Mountain	5.2 km (3.2 miles)/10.2 km (6.3 miles) roundtrip		•	•	•	•		
20. Centennial Seawall & Ambleside Park	6.4 km (4 miles) roundtrip	•		•	•	•	•	•
21. Capilano River Regional Park	About 17 km (10.5 miles) of trails	•	•	•	•	•		•
22. Grouse Grind	2.5 km (1.6 miles) one-way		•	•		•		•

Trail/Park	Distance	Walk	Hike	Run	Kids	Dogs	Bikes	Public Transit
23. Lynn Canyon Park	More than 11 km (7 miles) of trails	•	•	•	•	•		•
24. Lynn Headwaters Regional Park	More than 40 km (25 miles) of trails	•	•	•	•	•		•
25. Lower Seymour Conservation Reserve	More than 65 km (40 miles) of trails	•	•	•	•	partial	•	
26. Mount Seymour	8.4 km (5.2 miles) roundtrip		•	•	•	•		
EASTERN MUNICIPALITIES								
27. təmtəmíxʷtən/ Belcarra Regional Park	More than 26 km (16 miles) of trails	•	•	•	•	•		•
28. Mundy Park	16 km (10 miles) of trails	•	•	•	•	•	•	•
29. ƛ̓éxətəm Regional Park (Colony Farm)	11.8 km (7.3 miles) of trails	•	•	•	•	•	•	•
30. Minnekhada Regional Park	10.2 km (6.3 miles) of trails	•	•	•	•	•		
31. Pitt River Regional Greenway	11.3 km (7 miles) of trails	•	•	•	•	•	•	•
32. Kanaka Regional Park	11.8 km (7.3 miles) of trails	•	•	•	•	•		
RICHMOND & DELTA								
33. Iona Beach Regional Park	About 9 km (5.6 miles) of trails	•	•	•	•	•	•	
34. Richmond Nature Park	5 km (3.1 miles) of trails	•	•		•			•
35. West Dyke and Middle Arm Trails	10.8 km (6.7 miles) one-way	•	•	•	•	•	•	•

Trail/Park	Distance	Walk	Hike	Run	Kids	Dogs	Bikes	Public Transit
36. Steveston Greenway and South Dyke Trail	7.1 km (4.4 miles) one-way	•	•	•	•	•	•	•
37. Deas Island Regional Park	5.9 km (3.7 miles) of trails	•	•	•	•	•		•
38. Burns Bog Delta Nature Reserve	3.2-km (2-mile) loop	•	•		•	•		•
39. George C. Reifel Migratory Bird Sanctuary	About 4.5 km (2.8 miles) of trails	•	•		•			
40. Boundary Bay Regional Park	6 km (3.7 miles) of trails	•	•	•	•	•	•	•
41. Boundary Bay Dyke Trail	16.9 km (10.5 miles) one-way	•	•	•	•	partial	•	•
42. Lily Point Marine Park	3.5 km (2.2 miles) of trails	•	•	•	•	•	•	
SURREY & LANGLEY								
43. Surrey Bend Regional Park	6.8 km (4.2 miles) of trails	•	•	•	•	•	•	
44. Tynehead Regional Park	15 km (9.3 miles) of trails	•	•	•	•	•	•	•
45. Green Timbers Urban Forest Park	More than 16 km (10 miles) of trails	•	•	•	•	•	•	•
46. Crescent Beach & Blackie Spit	About 5 km (3.2 miles) of trails	•	•	•	•	partial		•
47. Crescent Park	About 8 km (5 miles) of trails	•	•	•	•	•		•
48. Sunnyside Acres Urban Forest	About 6 km (3.7 miles) of trails	•	•	•	•	•		•
49. Elgin HeritagePark	5.3 km (3.3 miles) of trails	•	•	•	•	•		•

Trail/Park	Distance	Walk	Hike	Run	Kids	Dogs	Bikes	Public Transit
50. Serpentine Fen	3.5 km (2.2 miles) round-trip	•	•	•	•	•		•
51. White Rock Promenade	4.4 km (2.7 miles) round-trip	•		•	•	partial		•
52. Campbell Valley Regional Park	33 km (20.5 miles) of trails	•	•	•	•	•	•	•
53. Derby Reach Regional Park	13 km (8.1 miles) of trails	•	•	•	•	•	•	•
54. Brae Island Regional Park	4.8-km (3-mile) loop	•	•	•	•	•	•	•
55. Aldergrove Regional Park	More than 15 km (9 miles) of trails	•	•	•	•	•	•	•

Next page: Totem poles at Stanley Park (Trail 1)

INTRODUCTION

VANCOUVER, BRITISH COLUMBIA, IS ONE of the most beautiful, vibrant, and livable cities not only in North America, but in the world. Situated at the mouth of the Fraser River on the Strait of Georgia and set against a backdrop of steep, craggy mountains, its location alone makes this an exceptional city. With nearly half of its residents born outside of Canada, Vancouver is one of the most culturally and ethnically diverse cities in Canada. With a population exceeding three million, the Metropolitan Vancouver area is home to some of the largest Chinese and Indian (particularly Sikh) populations in North America. The area is also home to communities of Japanese, Koreans, Southeast Asians, Filipinos, Pacific Islanders, Middle Easterners, Persians, First Nations, Latin Americans, Africans, and Europeans of British, Irish, Italian, German, Portuguese, Ukrainian, Romanian, and other ethnicities.

The Vancouver area lies within the traditional lands of ten local First Nations: Katzie, Kwantlen, Kwikwetlem, Matsqui, Musqueam, Qayqayt, Semiahmoo, Squamish, Tsawwassen, and Tsleil-Waututh. In 2015, the Metro Vancouver government committed to fostering respect, reconciliation, and mutual understanding with all Indigenous peoples and communities. Through reconciliation, Metro Vancouver is building and strengthening respectful and reciprocal relationships with local First Nations, engaging with them meaningfully on plans, programs, and projects. Metro Vancouver is committed to building trust through genuine collaboration, creating a mutually respectful space for meaningful dialogue and outcomes, and creating opportunities for Board-to-Nation relationships to thrive.

But aside from the city's rich heritage, natural environment, diverse population, and cultural offerings, what really makes this city such a livable place are its parks and trails. The Greater Vancouver area is blanketed with parks, traversed by trails, and ringed by natural areas. And Vancouver has a superb public transit system, allowing you to get to nearly all of those parks and trails sans car.

Urban Trails: Vancouver, BC focuses on the myriad of trails, parks, preserves, and greenbelts within the urban and suburban-fringe areas of the Metro Vancouver Regional District (MVRD) and the exclave of Point Roberts, Washington. The MVRD contains twenty-one municipalities, including the thriving cities of Surrey, Burnaby, Richmond, Coquitlam, and New Westminster—all equally as diverse and packed with parks and trails as Vancouver.

In this book you'll find trails to old-growth forests, lakeshores, coastal beaches, riverfronts, wildlife-rich wetlands, waterfalls, mountaintops, scenic vistas, meadows, historical sites, and vibrant neighborhoods and communities. While we often equate trails with wildernesses and forest areas, plenty of accessible trails and natural beauty are tucked away in population centers as well. The routes included here are designed to show you where you can go for a good run, long walk, or invigorating hike, right in the heart of Canada's third-largest metropolitan area.

This guide has two missions: to promote fitness and to advocate for outdoor recreation spaces in urban settings.

One of the best ways to get fit is to get outside more often! If Vancouver is your home, there is no need to take long trips to Whistler, the North Cascades, or the Rockies. You have a wide array of trails and parks right in your backyard or at the steps of your apartment or strata. These urban trails are available year-round, so you can walk, run, or hike every day within your own neighborhood. If you feel you are not getting outside enough or getting enough exercise, this book can help you achieve a healthier lifestyle.

If you're a visitor to Vancouver, this book aims to not only help you incorporate a little fitness and outdoor recreation into your holiday, but also show you the wide array of trails and parks the area has to offer.

Seawall Trail through David Lam Park (Trail 2)

WELCOME TO VANCOUVER

If you're visiting Vancouver from the States, then this section is for you.

There are four main border crossings in northwestern Washington: Peace Arch and Pacific Crossing (from Blaine to Surrey); Aldergrove (from Lynden to Langley); and Sumas (from Sumas to Abbotsford). All but Aldergrove are open twenty-four hours a day. Vancouver is also accessible from Washington via rail on the Amtrak Cascades line.

For overland border crossings, American citizens aged sixteen and older will need a valid passport, enhanced driver's license, or enhanced identity card. Visitors under the age of sixteen should also have proper identification—either a passport or a birth certificate. US citizens who frequently cross into Canada can apply for a NEXUS card, allowing for speedier border crossings through special lanes. Note that border crossings can be extremely busy during US/Canadian holiday periods.

What about dogs? All dogs older than three months, with the exception of certified assistance, hearing, or service dogs accompanying their user, must have proof of current rabies vaccination to enter Canada.

You can find more detailed information online about crossing the border at cbsa-asfc.gc.ca/travel-voyage/td-dv-eng.html.

DRIVING

Traffic can be tough in the MVRD, particularly in Vancouver, North Vancouver, and West Vancouver. Get familiar with the area's bridges (and Massey Tunnel), which are often the big traffic choke points in the region. However, the MVRD has an excellent public transit system called TransLink, and nearly all the destinations in this book can be reached via bus, SkyTrain, or ferry. One strategy I use to avoid driving in downtown Vancouver is to take the SkyTrain into the city from Richmond, Burnaby, New Westminster, Surrey, or Coquitlam. The SkyTrain also connects to the airport. You can find all metro transportation routes and information here: www.translink.ca.

CELL PHONES

You'll definitely want to use your cell phone for accessing metro info, park alerts, maps, and other travel information. Check with your provider about getting Canadian coverage prior to your trip or you could be in for some expensive roaming charges.

METRIC

Canada, like most of the world, uses the metric system. This guide shows all distances and elevations both in metric and imperial units. And note that a thirty-degree day in Canada is hot, not cold!

HOLIDAYS

As in the US, Canada and British Columbia (BC) celebrate New Year's, Labour Day, Remembrance Day (Veterans Day in US), and Christmas. Canada and BC also celebrate Good Friday (date varies), Victoria Day (last Monday preceding May 25), Canada Day (July 1), National Day for Truth and Reconciliation (Sept 30), and Thanksgiving (second Monday in October). And BC celebrates Family Day (third Monday in February) and British Columbia Day (first Monday in August). Border crossings can be extremely busy during these time periods.

SOME CANADIAN AND BC TERMS AND JARGON

You may want to familiarize yourself with these terms and phrases:
- **Clicks:** kilometer
- **First Nations:** Indigenous people in Canada that are not Métis or Inuit. BC is home to more than two hundred distinct First Nations.
- **Loonie:** Canada's one-dollar coin displaying a loon. Note that there are no dollar bills in use in Canada, nor pennies. All purchases are rounded up or down to the nearest nickel.
- **Lower Mainland:** region of British Columbia along the lower Fraser valley, including the Metro Vancouver Regional District and Fraser Valley Regional District.
- **New West:** New Westminster
- **North Van:** North Vancouver
- **PoCo:** acronym for Port Coquitlam
- **PoCoMo:** acronym for Port Coquitlam, Coquitlam, and Port Moody, collectively referred to as the Tri-Cities
- **PoMo:** acronym for Port Moody
- **SkyTrain:** TransLink's light rail, which consist of three lines: Canada, Expo, Millennium
- **Sleeve:** 16 fluid ounces (American pint) of beer
- **RCMP or Mounties:** Royal Canadian Mounted Police, Canada's national (federal) police
- **Tim's or Timmy's:** Tim Horton's, a ubiquitous Canadian coffee, donut, and sandwich shop
- **Toonie:** Canada's two-dollar coin
- **Washroom:** restroom
- **West Van:** West Vancouver

Mission number two of this guide is to promote the local parks, preserves, and trails that exist within and near our urban areas. Nearly three million people call the MVRD home. The region has seen explosive growth over the past few decades, and Vancouver is the country's most densely populated city.

While conservationists continue to promote protection of British Columbia's large tracts of wilderness and undeveloped lands—and that is important—it's equally important that we promote the preservation of natural areas and develop more trails and greenbelts right where people live. Why? For one thing, the MVRD and Lower Mainland contain unique and threatened ecosystems and areas of significance to the region's First Nations that deserve to be protected as much as our wilder remote places. And, we need to have accessible trails where people live, work, and spend the majority of their time. Urban trails and parks allow folks to regularly bond with nature and be outside. They help us cut our carbon footprint by giving us access to recreation without burning excessive amounts of fuel to reach a destination. They make it easier for us to commit to regular exercise programs, giving us safe and agreeable places to walk, run, and hike. And urban trails and parks also allow for people who may not have cars and/or the means to travel to wilderness provincial parks, crown lands, and national parks a chance to experience nature and a healthy lifestyle too. As the MVRD continues to grow, becoming increasingly crowded and more developed, it's all the more important that we support the expansion of more urban parks and trails.

So get out there, get fit, and have fun! And don't forget to advocate for more trails and parks.

HOW TO USE THIS GUIDE

THIS EASY-TO-USE GUIDE PROVIDES YOU with enough details to get out on the trail with confidence, while leaving enough room for your own personal discovery. I have walked, hiked, and/or run every kilometer of the trails described here, and the directions and advice are accurate and up to date. Conditions can and do change, however, so make sure you check on the status of a park or trail before you go. Each trail/park lists the managing agency to contact.

THE DESTINATIONS

This book includes fifty-five destinations, covering trails in and around Vancouver, West Vancouver, North Vancouver, Burnaby, New Westminster, Port Moody, Coquitlam, Port Coquitlam, Pitt Meadows, Maple Ridge, Richmond, Delta, Point Roberts, Surrey, White Rock, and Langley, as well as Bowen Island. It includes regional and provincial parks in the North Shore Mountains along the urban fringe of the metropolitan area, but it does not include backcountry trails from those destinations. Each of the included destinations begins with the park and/or trail name, followed by a block of information detailing the following:

Distance. Here you will find roundtrip distance (unless otherwise noted) if the route describes a single trail, or the total distance of trails within the park/preserve/greenway if the route gives an overview of the destination's trail system. Distances are given in both kilometers and miles. Note that while I have measured most of the trails in this book with GPS and have consulted maps and governing land agencies, the distance stated may not always be exact—but it'll be pretty darn close.

Elevation gain/high point. For individual trails, elevation gain (given in both meters and feet) is for the *cumulative* difference on the route (and return), meaning not only the difference between the high and low points on the trail, but also for all other significant changes in elevation along the way. For destinations where multiple routes are given, as in a trail network within a park, the elevation gain applies to the steepest trail on the route. The high point is the highest elevation of the trail or trail system described. Most of the trails in the book are at a relatively low elevation, ensuring mostly snow-free winter access.

Difficulty. This factor is based not only on length and elevation gain, but also on the type of tread and surface area of the trail(s). Most of the trails in this book are easy or moderate for the average hiker/walker/runner. Depending on your level of fitness, you may find the trails more or less difficult than described.

Fitness. This description denotes whether the trail is best for hikers, walkers, or runners. I also denote whether the trail is open to bicycles. Generally, paved trails will be of more interest to walkers and runners, while rough, hilly trails will appeal more to hikers. Of course, you are free to hike, walk, or run (unless running is specifically prohibited) on any of the trails in this book.

Family-friendly. Here you'll find notes on a trail's or park's suitability for children and any cautions to be aware

High points, like this summit of Mount Seymour, are provided at the beginning of each trail (Trail 26).

of, such as cliffs or heavy mountain bike use. Some trails may be noted as suitable for jogging strollers and/or wheelchair accessible.

Dog-friendly. This denotes whether dogs are allowed on the trail and what regulations (such as leashed and under control) apply. The MVRD contains many leash-free trails and areas. Trail users who are skittish around dogs may want to avoid these areas. Also, leash compliance in adjacent leash-required trails and areas tends to be low. Be a good trail user by abiding by park regulations. And if your dog is not well-behaved and under voice control, then it should be leashed.

Amenities. The featured park's amenities can include privies, drinking water, benches, interpretive signs/displays, shelters, picnic tables, learning centers, and campgrounds, to name a few.

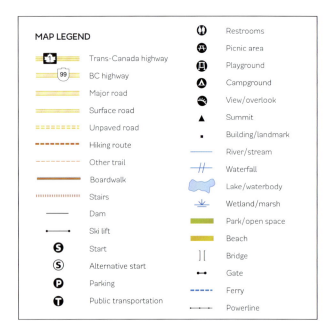

MAP LEGEND

Trans-Canada highway	Restrooms
BC highway	Picnic area
Major road	Playground
Surface road	Campground
Unpaved road	View/overlook
Hiking route	Summit
Other trail	Building/landmark
Boardwalk	River/stream
Stairs	Waterfall
Dam	Wetland/marsh
Ski lift	Park/open space
Start	Beach
Alternative start	Bridge
Parking	Gate
Public transportation	Ferry
	Powerline

(Legend also lists: Lake/waterbody)

Contact/maps. Here you'll find the route's managing agencies and where to get current trail conditions. All websites for trail and park managers or governing agencies can be found in the Resources. These websites will often direct you to trail and park maps; in some cases, a better or supplemental map is noted.

Before you go. This section notes any fees or permits required, hours the park or preserve is open (if limited), closures, and other special concerns.

GPS. GPS coordinates are provided for the main trailhead, to help get you to the trail.

GETTING THERE. Map to: Provides a trailhead, landmark, or other feature for you to enter into your map app on your phone (preferably Google Maps for best results) for precise driving directions from your location. **Transit:** Lists the

TransLink bus or SkyTrain line accessing the park or trailhead. **Parking:** I also provide parking information and some alternatives when available.

EACH DESTINATION CHAPTER begins with an overview of the featured park and/or trail, highlighting its setting and character, often with notes on the property's cultural, natural, and/or conservation history.

GET MOVING. This section describes the route or trails and what you might find on your hike, walk, or run; it may also note additional highlights beyond the trail itself, such as points of historical interest.

GO FARTHER. Here you'll find suggestions for making your hike/walk/run longer within the featured park—or perhaps by combining this trip with an adjacent park or trail.

PERMITS, REGULATIONS, AND PARK FEES

Most of the trails and parks described in this book are managed by city and regional district park divisions, requiring no permits or fees. Several MVRD parks, however, charge a seasonal parking fee (payable at self-pay stations). Vancouver's VanDusen Botanical Garden charges an admission fee. Some of the trails in this book are managed by BC Parks, which at times have entrance or parking fees or timed entry restrictions. Consult park websites before arriving for current parking guidelines. Regulations, such as whether dogs are allowed or a park has restricted hours or is closed for certain occasions, are clearly spelled out in the chapter information blocks.

PARK AND TRAIL CONDITIONS

In general, urban trails change little year to year. But changes can occur. A severe weather event can damage trails and park features. Windstorms can blow down multiple trees across trails, making paths impassable. Lack of adequate funding is also responsible for trail neglect and degradation. For some of the wilder destinations in this book, it is wise to contact the appropriate land manager after a significant weather event to check on current trail and road conditions.

OUTDOORS ETHICS

Strong, positive outdoors ethics include making sure you leave the trail (and park) in as good a condition as you found it—or even better. Get involved with groups and organizations that safeguard, watchdog, and advocate for land protection. And let land managers and public officials know how important protecting lands and trails is to you.

All of us who recreate in natural areas have a moral obligation and responsibility to respect and protect our natural heritage. Everything we do on the planet has an impact—and we should strive to have as little negative effect as possible. The **Leave No Trace** Center for Outdoors Ethics is an educational, nonpartisan, nonprofit organization that was developed for responsible enjoyment and active stewardship of the outdoors. Their program helps educate outdoor enthusiasts about their recreational impacts and recommends techniques to prevent and minimize such impacts. While geared toward backcountry use, many Leave No Trace (LNT) principles are sound advice for urban and urban-fringe parks too, including planning ahead, disposing of waste properly, and being considerate of other visitors. Visit lnt.org to learn more.

TRAIL ETIQUETTE

Trails and parks can be busy places, and we all need to get along. Some of the trails in this book are open to bikes and equestrians. When you encounter other trail users, whether they are hikers, runners, bicyclists, or horseback riders, follow common sense and exercise simple courtesy. With this Golden Rule of Trail Etiquette in mind, here are other things you can do during trail encounters to be a good trail user:

- **Observe the right-of-way.** Pedestrians have the right-of-way when encountering bicycles. However, on backcountry trails it is often difficult for bikers to stop. In these cases, those of us on foot should move off the trail. Hikers, walkers, and runners are more mobile and flexible, making it easier for us to quickly step off the trail. Many of Vancouver's busy trails have separate bike and pedestrian lanes. Be sure not to walk in the bike lanes. And stay to the right on shared trails, allowing faster hikers and runners and cyclists to safely pass.

- **Move aside for horses.** When meeting horseback riders, step off the downhill side of the trail unless the terrain makes this difficult or dangerous. In that case, move to the uphill side of the trail, but crouch down a bit so you do not tower over the horses' heads. Also, make yourself visible so as not to spook the big beasties, and talk in a normal voice to the riders. This calms the horses. If walking with a dog, keep your buddy under control.

- **Stay on trails.** Don't cut switchbacks, take shortcuts, or make new trails; all lead to erosion and unsightly trail degradation.

- **Obey the rules specific to the trail or park you are visiting.** Many trails are closed to certain types of use, including dogs and mountain bikes. Some trails are bike only—don't walk on them.

- **Keep dogs under control.** Trail users who bring dogs should have their dog on a leash or under very strict voice command at all times. And if leashes are required, then this *does* apply to you. Many trail users who have had negative encounters with dogs (actually with the dog owners) on the trail are not fond of, or are even afraid of, encountering dogs. Respect their right *not* to be approached by your darling pooch. A well-behaved leashed dog, however, can certainly help warm up these folks to a canine encounter. And always pack out your dog's poop and discard it properly. Many parks in the MVRD have designated receptacles for dog waste.

- **Avoid disturbing wildlife.** Observe from a distance, resisting the urge to move closer to wildlife (use your telephoto lens). This not only keeps you safer but also prevents the animal from having to exert itself unnecessarily to flee from you.
- **Take only photographs.** Leave all natural features and historical artifacts as you found them for others to enjoy.
- **Never roll rocks off trails or cliffs.** Gravity increases the impact of falling rocks exponentially, and you risk endangering lives below you.
- **Mind the music.** Not everyone (almost no one) wants to hear your blaring music. If you like listening to music while you run, hike, or walk, wear headphones and respect other trail users' right to peace and quiet—and to listen to nature's music.

BEARS AND COUGARS

British Columbia harbors healthy populations of black bears in many of the parks and preserves along the urban fringe. If you encounter a bear while you're on the trail, you'll usually just catch a glimpse of its bear behind. But occasionally the bruin may actually want to get a look at *you*.

To avoid an un-*bear*-able encounter, practice bear-aware prudence: Always keep a safe distance. Remain calm, do not look a bear in the eyes, speak in a low tone, and do not run from it. Hold your arms out to appear as big as possible. Slowly move away. The bear may bluff-charge—do not run. Usually, the bear will leave once he perceives he is not threatened. If he does attack, fight back using fists, rocks, trekking poles, or bear spray if you are carrying it.

A NOTE ABOUT SAFETY

BC also supports a healthy population of *Puma concolor*. While cougar encounters are extremely rare, they do occur— even occasionally in parks and preserves on the urban fringe. Cougars are cats—they're curious. They may follow hikers, but rarely (almost never) attack adult humans. Minimize contact by not hiking or running alone and by avoiding carrion. If you do encounter a cougar, remember the big cat is looking for prey that can't or won't fight back. Do not run, as this may trigger its prey instinct. Stand up and face it. If you appear aggressive, the cougar will probably back down. Wave your arms, trekking poles, or a jacket over your head to appear bigger, and maintain eye contact. Pick up children and small dogs and back away slowly if you can do so safely, not taking your eyes off of it. If it attacks, throw things at it. Shout loudly. If it gets close, whack it with your trekking pole, fighting back aggressively.

WATER AND GEAR

While most of the trails in this book can be enjoyed without much preparation or gear, it is always a good idea to bring water, even if you're just out for a quick walk or run. Even better, carry a small pack with water, a few snacks, sunglasses, and a rain jacket.

THE TEN ESSENTIALS

If you are heading out for a longer adventure—perhaps an all-day hike up Mount Gardner or Mount Seymour—pack the **Ten Essentials**, items that are good to have on hand in an emergency:

1. **Navigation.** Carry a map of the area you plan to be in and know how to read it. A cell phone and/or GPS unit are good to have along too.

2. **Headlamp.** If caught out after dark, you'll be glad you have a headlamp or flashlight so you can follow the trail home.

3. **Sun protection.** Even on wet days, carry sunscreen and sunglasses; you never know when the clouds will lift, and you can easily sunburn near water.

4. **First-aid supplies.** At the very least, your kit should include bandages, gauze, scissors, tape, tweezers, pain relievers, antiseptics, and perhaps a small manual.

5. **Knife.** A pocketknife or multitool can come in handy, as can basic repair items such as nylon cord, safety pins, a small roll of duct tape, and a small tube of superglue.

6. **Fire.** While being forced to spend the night out is not likely on these trails, a campfire could provide welcome warmth in an emergency, with matches kept dry in a zip-top bag.

7. **Shelter.** This can be as simple as a garbage bag or a rain poncho that can double as an emergency tarp.

8. **Extra food.** Pack a handful of nuts or sports bars for emergency pick-me-ups.

9. **Extra water.** Bring enough water to keep you hydrated, and for longer treks consider a means of water purification.

10. **Extra clothes.** Storms can and do blow in rapidly. Carry raingear, wind gear, and extra layers.

TRAIL CONCERNS

By and large, Vancouver's parks and trails are safe places. Common sense and vigilance, however, are still in order. This is true for all trail users, but especially for solo ones. Be aware of your surroundings at all times. Let someone know when and where you're headed out.

Sadly, car smash-and-grabs are a common occurrence at some parks and trailheads. Absolutely under no circumstances leave anything of value in your vehicle while out on the trail. Take your wallet and smartphone with you. A duffel bag on the back seat may contain dirty T-shirts, but a thief may think there's a laptop in it. Save yourself the hassle of returning to a busted window by not giving criminals a reason to clout your car.

Safety can be a concern at some urban parks. It's best to stay on established trails and leave the area if you feel uncomfortable. Where homelessness is an issue, be aware of needles, human waste, and other debris. Parks and trails where this is a serious concern have been omitted from this book.

No need to be paranoid, though, for Vancouver's trails and parks are fairly safe places. Just use a little common sense and vigilance while you're out and about.

Next page: Seawall Trail through Charlson Park (Trail 2)

VANCOUVER

Founded on the ancestral lands of the Musqueam, Squamish, and Tsleil-Waututh peoples, Vancouver began as a small community called Gastown, established shortly after the Confederation of Canada in 1867, that was centered around a mill and a saloon. It has since grown into one of the world's great cities. With a population nearing 750,000, Vancouver is Canada's eighth-largest city, and its metropolitan area is the third largest in the country.

Vancouver also has the highest population density in the country (the fourth highest in North America) and is one of the most expensive cities in the world to live in, yet it consistently ranks as one of the most livable cities in the world. It is ethnically and culturally diverse, has an excellent public transportation system, and is teeming with cultural attractions, parks, greenbelts, and an extensive urban trail system. The city's urban planning places a strong emphasis on aesthetics and view corridors. It is bike-friendly and has one of the largest public waterfronts of any major metropolis. Much of Vancouver's industrial past has been and continues to be transformed into livable neighborhoods complete with greenbelts and trails.

Owing to its excellent public transportation system and network of trails, Vancouver is easy to explore on foot. Its beautiful parks, breathtaking natural surroundings, and culturally dynamic neighborhoods make Vancouver one of the finest destinations in the world when it comes to urban hiking, walking, and running.

1 Stanley Park

DISTANCE:	More than 27 km (17 miles) of trails
ELEVATION GAIN:	Up to 152 m (500 feet)
HIGH POINT:	84 m (275 feet)
DIFFICULTY:	Easy
FITNESS:	Walkers, runners, hikers, bicyclists
FAMILY-FRIENDLY:	Yes, and several trails wheelchair- and jogging stroller–friendly
DOG-FRIENDLY:	On leash
AMENITIES:	Washrooms, water, picnic tables and shelters, concessions, playground, sports fields, pools, aquarium, gardens, sports courts, spray park, public art, sculptures, totem poles
CONTACT/MAPS:	City of Vancouver Parks, Recreation, and Cultural Services
BEFORE YOU GO:	Open from 6:00 AM to 10:00 PM; park can be extremely busy and crowded at times. Adhere to directional and usage signs. Parking can be challenging on weekends and in summer—consider taking public transportation.
GPS:	N49.299 W123.122

GETTING THERE

Map to: Stanley Park Drive, Vancouver, BC. **Transit:** TransLink buses 19, 44, 240, 241, 246, 247, 250, 253, 254, 257, N24. **Parking:** You'll find many pay parking lots (easypark.ca) and trailheads on 9-km (5.6-mile) Stanley Park Road. Alternative pay parking areas and trailheads can be found on other park roads.

Vancouver's crown jewel, Stanley Park rivals New York's Central Park as one of the most beautiful, popular, and loved urban parks in the world. Occupying 405 ha (1000 acres) at the tip of the Burrard Peninsula within the shadows of the city's downtown core, Stanley Park's dense canopy of towering evergreens is striking against rows of steel-and-glass towers. Although peppered with statues, attractions, and

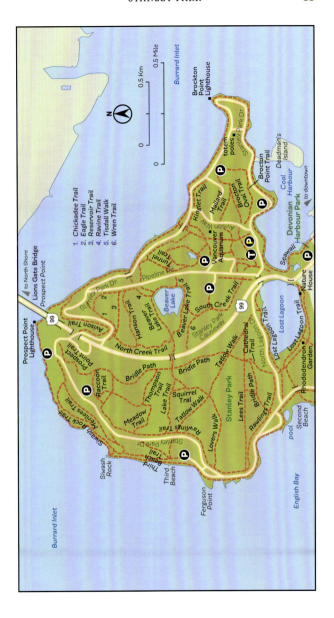

Burrard Inlet

Burrard Inlet

to North Shore

Lions Gate Bridge
Prospect Point

Prospect Point
Lighthouse

Brockton
Point
Lighthouse

Burrard Inlet

Brockton
Point Trail

Deadman's
Island

Coal
Harbour

Devonian
Harbour Park

Seawall

to downtown

1. Chickadee Trail
2. Eagle Trail
3. Reservoir Trail
4. Ravine Trail
5. Tisdall Walk
6. Wren Trail

totem
poles

Stanley Park Dr

Brockton
Oval Trail

Kinglet Trail

Mallard
Trail

Avison Walk

Vancouver
Aquarium

Tunnel Trail

Pipeline Rd.

Stanley Park Dr

Avison Trail

Beaver
Lake

Beaver Lake Trail

Hanson Trail

Beaver Lake Trail

South Creek Trail

South Creek Trail

Stanley Park
Causeway

99

99

Nature
House

Lost Lagoon

Lost Lagoon Trail

Lost Lagoon Trail

North Lagoon Trail

North Lagoon Trail

North Creek Trail

Bridle Path

Bridle Path

Tatlow Walk

Cathedral
Trail

Prospect
Point Trail

Raccoon
Trail

Siwash Rock Trail

Merilees Trail

Bridle Path

Thompson
Trail

Lake Trail

Squirrel
Trail

Tatlow Walk

Meadow
Trail

Rawlings Trail

Lovers Walk

Stanley Park

Lees Trail

Bridle Path

Rawlings Trail

Rhododendron
Garden

pool

Second
Beach

Stanley Park Dr

Beach Trail

Third
Beach

Siwash
Rock

Ferguson
Point

English Bay

0.5 Mile

0.5 Km

N

sporting and cultural facilities, most of this sprawling park remains in a natural state. A large network of trails leads to its quiet forest groves, wildlife-rich interior waterways, and scenic viewpoints of sea, city, and summits.

GET MOVING

Unlike many of the great urban parks of North America, Stanley was not designed by a landscape-architect firm like the Olmsted Brothers. It started as a military reserve in 1863 in preparation for an American attack on New Westminster (the capital of British Columbia at the time), despite it already containing First Nations and settler populations. Shortly afterward, Edward Stamp established a mill here and logging operations commenced.

In 1886, the newly incorporated city of Vancouver moved to establish the reserve as a public park—and two years later it became a reality. The park was named for Lord Stanley, governor general of Canada at the time (and whom the National Hockey League's coveted Stanley Cup is also named for). In 1889, Stanley officially dedicated the park "to the use and enjoyment of peoples of all colours, creeds, and customs, for all time." I could write an entire book just on this park. It has a rich history and multifaceted terrain, and you will enjoy discovering it all. The more developed areas of the park are in its southern reaches. The forested interior trails are less used than the paved exterior paths. Below is a sampling of some suggested routes for hikes, runs, and walks to get you started exploring this amazing park.

The Seawall is the most popular trail in the park. Scads of folks from all over the world and all walks of life—during all hours of the day and all year-round—walk, run, in-line skate, or bike this paved path hugging the park's scenic shoreline on Burrard Inlet and English Bay. The Seawall travels for 9 km (5.6 miles) in the park and is counterclockwise-only, with separate lanes for pedestrians and cyclists. (See Trail 2 for a detailed description of this route.) By using the paved Lost Lagoon Trail from Second Beach, you can make a 9.5-km (5.9-mile) loop. Pass by the park's Nature House and Rhododendron Garden on this trail. And look for birds in the lagoon, which was once a tidal marsh. Herons and eagles nest in the park.

A shorter loop can be made on the Seawall by following it from Coal Harbour, traveling around Brockton Point to the Ravine Trail at 3.8 km (2.4 miles). Then follow this wheelchair-accessible trail 0.3 km (0.2 mile) to Beaver Lake.

Hiker on Ravine Trail as it leads to Beaver Lake

Continue left on the Beaver Lake Trail to the South Creek Trail, passing through the gorgeous Rose Garden and returning to your start at 5.8 km (3.6 miles).

An out-and-back trip from the Seawall along the Ravine Trail and around Beaver Lake is 1.6 km (1 mile). The lake, which is surrounded by tall timber, covered with flowering lilies, and hopping with vocal invasive bullfrogs, is quite pretty.

Most of the park's wide, soft-surface interior trails are former skid rows from when the park was logged. The Rawlings Trail, Bridle Path, Lovers Walk, and Prospect Point Trail west of the Stanley Park Causeway (BC 99) can be combined for some great running loops of up to 6.5 km (4 miles). Due to a recent hemlock looper moth infestation, the Vancouver Park Board has approved logging nearly a quarter of the park's affected trees A controversial decision, it is currently being met with growing criticism and opposition.

The 1.5-km (0.9-mile) Tatlow Walk travels past some of the park's oldest and biggest trees, some up to 76 m (250 feet) tall. You can access this trail from the Third Beach parking lot or from trails along Lost Lagoon. The Merilees Trail takes off north from the Third Beach parking lot to the Siwash Rock Trail, from which you can view Siwash Rock, an iconic landmark along the Seawall (and the subject of a Squamish story), from above. Views are also excellent out across Burrard Inlet—excellent enough that this spot housed a gun battery during World War I and a military watchtower (which still remains) in the 1930s. A bunker was also built at Ferguson Point to the south. You can continue on the rolling Siwash Rock Trail back to the Merilees Trail for a short 3.2-km (2-mile) loop. Or head to Prospect Point, with its excellent view of the majestic Lions Gate Bridge, and return on the Prospect Point, Rawlings, and Third Beach Trails for a 4.2-km (2.6-mile) loop.

Have fun exploring this park on many return visits.

2   Seawall

DISTANCE:	22.8 km (14.2 miles) one-way
ELEVATION GAIN:	Minimal
HIGH POINT:	12 m (40 feet)
DIFFICULTY:	Easy
FITNESS:	Walkers, runners, bicyclists
FAMILY-FRIENDLY:	Yes, and wheelchair- and jogging stroller–friendly
DOG-FRIENDLY:	On leash
AMENITIES:	Washrooms, water, benches, concessions, playgrounds, gardens, interpretive signs, public art, sculptures, totem poles
CONTACT/MAPS:	City of Vancouver Parks, Recreation, and Cultural Services
BEFORE YOU GO:	Street parking is extremely limited along Seawall. Stanley Park, Vanier Park, and Kitsilano Beach Park offer the best options for parking. Consider public transportation.
GPS:	N49.288 W123.115

GETTING THERE

Map to: Vancouver Convention Centre, Vancouver, BC. **Transit to Stanley Park:** TransLink 19, 44, 240, 241, 246, 247, 250, 253, 254, 257, N24. **To points along Seawall:** TransLink 3, 23, 50; SkyTrain Expo Line stops at Burrard near the Seawall start and at Stadium-Chinatown near False Creek. **To Kitsilano Beach Park:** TransLink line 2. **Parking:** You'll find many pay parking lots adjacent to the Seawall on 9-km (5.6-mile) Stanley Park Drive. Visit easypark.ca for location and rate information for other nearby parking lots.

One of the longest continuous urban waterfront paths in the world, the Seawall takes you on a 22.8-km (14.2-mile) odyssey through beautiful city landscapes. Pass shiny, towering offices and residences; tree-lined, rocky Stanley Park shoreline; vibrant greenbelt parks and neighborhoods along False Creek; and gorgeous lawns and sandy beaches bustling with activity. And from every point along the way, savor jaw-dropping maritime, mountainous, and metropolitan views.

GET MOVING

Folks from throughout the city and the world flock to the Seawall year-round. It can get downright crowded on summer days and evenings. Separate lanes exist for foot and wheeled traffic, making the Seawall safer and more enjoyable for all

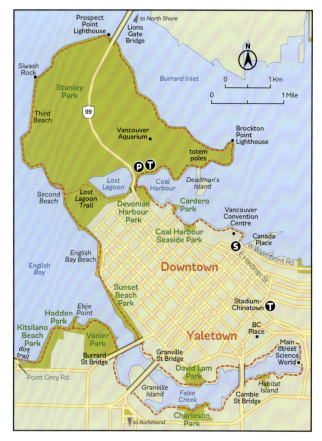

users. Note, too, that in Stanley Park, from Coal Harbour to Second Beach, travel on the Seawall is counterclockwise-only.

To mitigate erosion along Stanley Park's foreshore, construction of the Seawall (a stone wall which would eventually include a paved path upon it) began in 1917 and wasn't officially completed until 1980. The Vancouver Park Board's master stonemason, James Cunningham, oversaw much of its work for thirty-five years. The Seawall in Stanley Park is often referred to as the Cunningham Seawall. Since 1980, it has been greatly extended, from the Vancouver Convention Centre on Vancouver Harbour to Kitsilano Beach Park on English Bay. While strong runners and walkers can complete the entire Seawall in one swoop, it makes for great shorter outings anywhere along the way. And with public transportation, it's easy to do one-way trips. Below is a brief description of the entire route, from start to finish.

The Seawall starts by the Vancouver Convention Centre on West Waterfront Road, just to the west of the massive, iconic Canada Place, a convention center and cruise ship terminal designed like a boat. The Seawall passes *The Drop*, the first of many intriguing works of art along the way, and then bends west, passing a slew of delectable eateries and a busy seaplane center on Vancouver Harbour. The way passes a couple of marinas and a hotel and travels through historic Coal Harbour Seaside Park and Cardero Park, with its sea bridge granting excellent views of Coal Harbour.

The Seawall traverses Devonian Harbour Park with its off-leash area and comes to a junction at 2.2 km (1.4 miles) just before entering massive Stanley Park (Trail 1).

Continue into Vancouver's showpiece park, passing rowing and yacht club docks and a causeway (closed to public) to little Deadman's Island, a former burial ground turned naval reserve. The trail continues east, passing statues and historical relics before rounding Brockton Point with its well-photographed, 1914-built lighthouse. Now head

Seawall Trail in Stanley Park near Siwash Rock

northwest, passing a spray park, more statues and points of historical interest, and trails to Stanley Park's excellent totem pole collection and the Vancouver Aquarium.

The way becomes more scenic, with large trees lining the way and excellent views across the First Narrows of Burrard Inlet to North Shore peaks. After passing beneath the eloquent 1937-built Lions Gate Bridge, the Seawall comes to the 1948-built Prospect Point Lighthouse. Now travel along the base of bluffs to Siwash Rock, a scenic sea stack and the subject of a Squamish First Nations legend.

At 8.9 km (5.5 miles), come to Third Beach, the first of many good beaches along English Bay. At 10.4 km (6.5 miles), just past the Second Beach pool, the Lost Lagoon Trail takes off east. It is possible to complete a popular 9.5-km (5.9-mile) loop around Stanley Park by following this trail as it hugs Lost Lagoon's southern shore before reaching the Seawall once again after 1.3 km (0.8 mile). For now, continue south on the Seawall, leaving Stanley Park for popular English Bay Beach before traversing the long green swath of Sunset Beach

Park. Pass under the Burrard and Granville Street Bridges and begin wrapping around False Creek, a narrow inlet in the heart of the city. All along False Creek, pass docks used by False Creek Ferries (granvilleislandferries.bc.ca). These passenger ferries allow you to make a loop around False Creek instead of backtracking.

The Seawall continues through the hip Yaletown neighborhood, passing many wonderful waterfront parks, public art pieces, and points of historical interest. Pass under the Cambie Street Bridge and gaze across to the BC Place stadium, proceeding through former industrial areas that are now parks. At 16.6 km (10.3 miles), reach the attractive Science World complex at False Creek's terminus. The way then bends west, hugging the inlet's south shore and traversing more inviting greenbelts.

At 17.4 km (10.8 miles), pass a spur leading to Habitat Island, a small natural spot in the inlet. The Seawall then passes under the Cambie Street Bridge once again, skirting marinas and traversing the treed Charleson Park with its pond, garden, off-leash dog area, and great views of the downtown skyline. At 19.6 km (12.2 miles), reach a trail leading to Granville Island, which is actually a peninsula. A former industrial area, Granville Island is now a popular shopping and arts district with a public market. The Seawall continues west under the Granville Street Bridge, passing more marinas and a slew of wharfs. At 20.5 km (12.7 miles), walk through the Cultural Harmony Grove and dart under the Burrard Street Bridge.

The Seawall then enters the 17-ha (42-acre) Vanier Park, transitioning away from the high-density urban landscape of False Creek. Follow a wide dirt path along the mouth of the inlet, passing small ponds and open fields. Side trails head for the Museum of Vancouver and Planetarium Star Theatre and other park points of interest. The Seawall path skirts the Maritime Museum and enters Hadden Park, where a short spur leads to Elsje Point, granting stunning views across English Bay to downtown Vancouver's skyline and Stanley Park.

At 21.8 km (13.5 miles), the Seawall path enters Kitsilano Beach Park. On warm, sunny days when scads of folks are playing beach volleyball, paddling, and sunbathing, Kitsilano (Kits to the locals) Beach gives off a California vibe. Continue along sandy beaches and groves of towering trees and pass the park's large saltwater pool. At 22.8 km (14.2 miles), come to the Seawall's end at the Kitsilano Yacht Club. A narrow path along the shore beneath rows of homes continues for another 0.3 km (0.2 mile) to Point Grey Road.

3 Jericho, Locarno & Spanish Banks Beach Parks

DISTANCE:	4 km (2.5 miles) of beach; about 7.5 km (4.7 miles) of trails
ELEVATION GAIN:	Up to 90 m (300 feet)
HIGH POINT:	30 m (100 feet)
DIFFICULTY:	Easy
FITNESS:	Walkers, hikers, runners
FAMILY-FRIENDLY:	Yes, and several trails wheelchair- and jogger stroller–friendly
DOG-FRIENDLY:	On leash in park; prohibited on beach. Off-leash area at Spanish Banks.
AMENITIES:	Water, washrooms, benches, interpretive signs, trailhead bike racks, concessions, hostel, picnic area, sports fields, beach volleyball
CONTACT/MAPS:	City of Vancouver Parks, Recreation, and Cultural Services
BEFORE YOU GO:	Jericho Beach is a happening place, with festivals and sporting events year-round; consult website for schedule.
GPS:	N49.275 W123.202

0.5 Mile

0.5 Km

0

0

N

English Bay

Royal Vancouver Yacht Club

trail on sidewalk

Point Grey Rd

to 99

Hastings Mill Park

to 99

Jericho Beach Park

W 4th Ave

Jericho Lands

Jericho Beach Kayak Centre

Jericho Sailing Centre

S

P

Jericho Pier

Locarno Beach

hostel

Trimble St

W 4th Ave

W 8th Ave

Tolmie St

Waterfront Trail

NW Marine Dr

Spanish Banks Creek

Spanish Banks off-leash dog area

P

P

Canyon Creek

Pacific Spirit Regional Park

Chancellor Blvd

Acadia Beach trailhead

GETTING THERE
Map to: Jericho Beach Public Tennis Courts, Vancouver, BC.
Transit: TransLink buses 4, 42, 44, 84. **Parking:** Jericho Beach
Park has a pay parking lot. Free street parking and small lots
are available along NW Marine Drive abetting Locarno Beach
and Spanish Banks Beach Parks.

Jericho, Locarno, and Spanish Banks form a continuous 4-km
strand of sandy beaches along the south shore of Burrard Inlet.
Some of Vancouver's finest and most popular beaches, the
trio also ranks among the nicest urban beaches in the entire
Pacific Northwest. Views of Vancouver's shimmering skyline,
craggy North Shore summits, and glistening, vessel-busy
waterways are breathtaking. While these beaches attract
scads of sun worshippers and beachcombers, they're also
fitness havens. The waters teem with paddlers, the beaches
with volleyball players, and the trails with walkers, cyclists, and
runners of all sizes, ages, and abilities—especially runners. It's
one of the city's most popular running destinations.

GET MOVING
Most of the pedestrian action is on the wide and hard-packed
Waterfront Trail, which runs for 3.9 km (2.4 miles)—all the
way from Point Grey Road at Jericho Beach's eastern end
through Locarno Beach and Spanish Banks Beach—before
terminating just a short distance from the Acadia Beach trailhead in Pacific Spirit Regional Park (see Trail 4). Parts of the
trail have separate lanes for pedestrians and cyclists, so pay
attention to help keep a smooth traffic flow. Paralleling NW
Marine Drive, the Waterfront Trail heads west from Jericho
Beach (named not for the biblical city but for an early log-
ger) through a green swath graced with stately trees before
entering Locarno Beach (named after a peace pact signed in
Switzerland after World War I). Locarno is the site of the oldest Indigenous settlement on the Point Grey Peninsula.

Runners in Jericho Beach Park against a backdrop of North Shore Mountains

Pass one fine stretch of sandy beach after another, some usually bustling with volleyball tournaments. Views are breathtaking, especially east to downtown Vancouver, Stanley Park, and the Lions Gate Bridge. The trail then enters Spanish Banks Beach Park (named in honor of Spanish explorer José María Narváez, the first European to sail into Burrard Inlet) and after crossing Spanish Banks Creek on a bridge, enters a more natural area. Here Pacific Spirit Regional Park's mature forests replace the previous rows of tony houses. The trail continues west, entering a popular off-leash dog area and dog beach before reaching its end at a viewpoint granting spectacular vistas out to Bowen Island and Point Atkinson (Lighthouse Park) at the head of Howe Sound.

While the Waterfront Trail is among the most scenic in Vancouver, it can be crowded. If you're looking for more peaceful wanderings, there are several kilometers of inter-connecting trails within the 16.7 ha (115 acre) Jericho Beach Park. You can create several loops through the upland for-est and around the large duck pond and marsh in the park.

And the beach itself is one of the finest in Vancouver to walk. You'll just need to walk around the Jericho Beach Kayak Centre and Jericho Sailing Centre along the way.

GO FARTHER

During low tides, you can continue walking west on the beach to Acadia Beach and Wreck Beach (Trail 5).

At the Waterfront Trail's eastern terminus, you can walk on the sidewalk along Point Grey Road for 0.4 km (0.25 mile) to the small Hastings Mill Park. Here, check out Vancouver's oldest structure, the 1865-built Hastings Mill company store. Moved from its original spot in 1930, the building once also served as Vancouver's (then Granville's) first post office and general store. It now serves as a museum. Also consider spending a night at Jericho Beach's HI Canada hostel. The rates are affordable, but the place can be busy.

4 Pacific Spirit Regional Park

DISTANCE:	More than 55 km (34 miles) of trails
ELEVATION GAIN:	Up to 90 m (300 feet)
HIGH POINT:	85 m (280 feet)
DIFFICULTY:	Easy to moderate
FITNESS:	Walkers, runners, hikers
FAMILY-FRIENDLY:	Yes, and several trails wheelchair- and jogging stroller–friendly
DOG-FRIENDLY:	Some trails off leash and controlled; others only on leash. No dogs on weekends and statutory holidays on several trails near Park Centre on 16th Ave.
AMENITIES:	Water, washrooms, benches, interpretive signs
CONTACT/MAPS:	Metro Vancouver Regional Parks
BEFORE YOU GO:	Several trails open to bikes and horses
GPS:	N49.259 W123.223

GETTING THERE

Map to: Pacific Spirit Regional Park, Park Centre Parking Lot, Vancouver, BC. **Transit:** TransLink buses 4, 9, 14, 25, 33, 44, 49, 84, R4 (rapid line), 99B-Line (express line). **Parking:** Find parking at Park Centre or street parking. The lot on W. 16th Avenue is small but has two electric vehicle charging stations. Ample (except on sunny weekends) free parking along W. 16th Avenue and SW Marine Drive. Adjacent UBC parking areas require payment.

Vancouver's largest park, Pacific Spirit is nearly twice the size of Stanley Park, but without the developments of a big city park. Occupying a large swath of land on the Point Grey Peninsula, Pacific Spirit Regional Park separates the sprawling University of British Columbia (UBC) campus from the city. Originally part of University Endowment Lands, Pacific Spirit was established as a park in 1989, to be managed mainly as a natural forest preserve. More than 55 km (34 miles) of trails (34 km of them open to bicycles and horses) traverse the 763-ha (1885-acre) park. While most of the park consists of mature second-growth forest, there are some interesting features, including secluded beaches, several headland ravines, a rich bog, a few small creeks, and a few remnant ancient grand firs. And while the park can be busy, it rarely feels crowded with its large network of trails.

GET MOVING

Pacific Spirit Regional Park is separated into three units: the south and north units are divided by University Boulevard, while the west unit encompasses the foreshore and Wreck Beach, separated from the rest of the park by SW Marine Drive. (See Trail 5, Wreck Beach, for a description of the west unit.) Of the two non-coastal sections, the south unit offers more trails and is far busier than the north unit. Park maps show the two units at different scales, giving the north unit the appearance of being much smaller than the south. While the north unit offers fewer trails, they are less traveled and have more elevation change, providing more variety and a better workout.

The park's trail system is well marked with location maps at many of the junctions. Trails vary from wide, old service roads to narrower, hiking-only paths. Be aware that most of the park is leash optional, and even on the trails that require leashes, adherence is dismal. If you don't care to be around dogs, you may want to bypass this park, as it's extremely popular with canine-accompanied hikers and walkers. All dogs, of course, should be under control at all times.

Pacific Spirit offers many loop options, allowing you to cater your hike, run, or walk from a short afternoon stroll to an all-day outing. Privies are located at many of the main park access points as well as at Camosun Bog. Paved trails that run parallel to W. 16th Avenue and SW Marine Drive, popular with students and commuters, are good for tying loops together.

Most of the trails are multiuse, but there are more hiker-only trails in the north unit. The 6.5-km (4-mile) Salish Trail connects the two units, traversing them north to south. A periphery hike around the south unit along various trails is around 10 km (6.2 miles). A periphery hike around the north unit is around 5.5 km (3.4 miles). The Sword Fern, Imperial, Salish, and SW Marine Trails flank the 90-ha (222-acre) Ecological Preserve No. 74, which is used for forest research and is not open to the public. But you can peer into it as you walk around it.

Camosun Bog, located east of Imperial Drive in the south unit, is perhaps the park's most intriguing feature. Formed over ten thousand years ago from retreating glaciers, Camosun has been a sphagnum bog for the past two thousand years. The bog is sacred to the area's Indigenous people, the Musqueam. Elders tell of a small lake within the bog

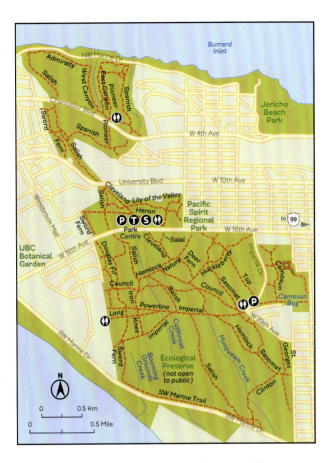

that gave origin to a double-headed serpent. The serpent was so large that its slithering created a path that became Musqueam Creek. From the serpent's droppings, a sacred river grass called the məθkʷəẏ grew, and the Musqueam became known as the people of the river grass.

During much of the twentieth century, the bog was altered and degraded by encroaching development. A large consortium has since been working to restore this fragile and special ecosystem. A series of wheelchair-accessible boardwalks with interpretive signs allows you to explore this area and view its rare plants, including carnivorous sundews. Park along West 29th Avenue and hike the Top and Camosun Trails for 1 km (0.6 mile) to access the bog.

GO FARTHER

The adjacent UBC Botanical Garden (entrance fee) is definitely worth a visit. Wander on a series of trails across its 44 ha (110 acres), admiring more than eight thousand plant species, with an emphasis on Pacific Northwest and Asian plants. The garden's thrilling Greenheart TreeWalk allows you to appreciate mature northwest forest from a new perspective, walking along platforms and suspension bridges up to 23 m (75 feet) above the forest floor.

Pacific Spirit's towering second growth forest

5   Wreck Beach

DISTANCE:	More than 5 km (3 miles) of beach; about 2.5 km (1.5 miles) of trails
ELEVATION GAIN:	Up to 90 m (300 feet)
HIGH POINT:	85 m (280 feet)
DIFFICULTY:	Easy to moderate
FITNESS:	Walkers, hikers
FAMILY-FRIENDLY:	Yes
DOG-FRIENDLY:	From Acadia Beach to Trail 6, dogs permitted (leash optional) Oct 1–Feb 28; prohibited Mar 1–Sept 30. Prohibited year-round from Trail 6 to Trail 7.
AMENITIES:	Water, washrooms, benches, interpretive signs, trailhead bike racks
CONTACT/MAPS:	Metro Vancouver Regional Parks
BEFORE YOU GO:	Wreck Beach is clothing optional; be prepared to see some flesh and respect the privacy of fellow beachgoers. Beach between Point Grey and Acadia Beach is rocky and can be difficult to travel; only attempt during low tides.
GPS:	N49.253 W123.251

GETTING THERE

Map to: UBC Botanical Garden, Vancouver, BC. **Transit:** TransLink bus 68 stops near Trail 3, 4, 6, and 7 trailheads. TransLink buses R4, 4, 9, 14, 23, 25, 44, 49, 68, 84, 99 service the UBC Exchange, which is a 0.8-km (0.5-mile) walk from Trail 3. **Parking:** For Trail 4 and Trail 6, find street parking and a paid parking lot on SW Marine Drive. For Trail 7, street parking is on Old Marine Drive. A small parking area on NW Marine Drive is near the Acadia Beach trailhead. Parking areas fill on sunny days. Alternative pay parking lots on UBC campus.

Vancouver's famed Wreck Beach has a long and storied history. Traditional land of the Musqueam people, this stretch of beach on Grey Peninsula just north of the Fraser River Delta provided excellent crabbing. In the 1920s on the adjacent bluff

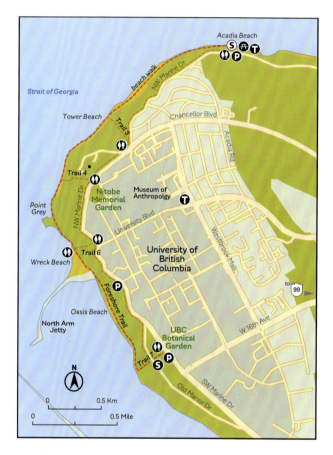

top, University Endowment Lands construction commenced, developing the University of British Columbia (UBC) campus. Old ships were sunk at the beach to create a breakwater, facilitating the arrival of construction materials via sea. The wrecked ships gave the beach its name. Nude bathing at the secluded beach began in the 1920s, growing more popular with the counterculture movement of the 1960s and '70s. In 1989, Wreck Beach became part of Pacific Spirit Regional

Park. Two years later, it was officially sanctioned as a clothing-optional beach.

GET MOVING

Wreck Beach can be a very busy place, especially the sandy stretches between Trail 6 and Point Grey. The rockier coastline north of Point Grey is much quieter—you can expect far fewer folks, especially during the wet and cold months. During most of the year, expect plenty of clothes-free beachgoers. Wet, cold days are best if you prefer to hike primarily among "textiles" (a term given to clothed beachgoers by nudists).

There are five access points to the beach: the Acadia Beach trailhead (near the north unit of Pacific Spirit Regional Park) and Trails 3, 4, 6, and 7 (named after nearby UBC parking lots). All four of these numbered trails are short but require steep descents (ascents on the return) in forested ravines via a series of up to five hundred stairs. Trail 6 is the most popular, with direct access to Wreck's sandiest section.

A one-way walk along the coastline of the entire route can be made into a loop by retuning on paved paths through the UBC campus above the beaches. This loop can start from any of the trailheads, but is described here from south to north, starting at Trail 7. After descending steps through a ravine alongside a small creek, emerge on a forested flat. The beach and parkland south of here are closed for environmental restoration and cultural preservation.

Start hiking north on the Foreshore Trail on a rough-at-times course. The way can be muddy and slick, especially during the winter. Skirting the base of steep bluffs, the way passes some big old-growth trees. The beach referred to here as Oasis is primarily composed of mudflats and calm coves created by the long North Arm Jetty. Log booms line the channel. Stay on the main trail here and avoid side trails to secluded spots that are occasionally used for illicit hookups.

Beach near Point Grey

The trail emerges along the edge of a large, grassy cove excellent for bird-watching before reaching the heart of Wreck Beach at Trail 6 at 1.4 km (0.9 mile). Here enjoy a wide, sandy beach created by a small jetty. This area can get downright crowded, complete with group activities and sanctioned vendors during the summer. Privies can be found near the trail junction.

Continue walking north, mainly on sandy beach, rounding Point Grey and some steep, unstable bluffs. The beach bends eastward and becomes rockier, with pockets of sand. The route uses shoreline and short trails bypassing ledges. At 2.2 km (1.4 miles), pass by Trail 4 and continue on a beautiful stretch of coastline referred to as Tower Beach due to its two old and graffiti-covered World War II signal towers. At 3 km (1.9 miles), reach Trail 3 at the second tower.

Continuing north, the way is rocky and slow going, but the views are lovely north to Bowen Island, North Shore peaks, Howe Sound, the mouth of Burrard Inlet, and across the Strait of Georgia. Shoreline vegetation here is thick and jungle-like. At 4.1 km (2.6 miles), come to Acadia Beach and a trail heading right. You can continue along the beach, soon reaching a trail leading to a picnic area before coming to the Acadia Beach trailhead at 4.5 km (2.8 miles).

To return to the Trail 7 trailhead, take the trail leading right (south) from the beach and start climbing through forest, then meadow, before reaching a paved path paralleling NW Marine Drive. Continue right, ascending and reaching the sprawling UBC campus. Continue walking along NW Marine Drive on paved and soft-surface paths, arriving at the Trail 7 trailhead after 8.8 km (5.5 miles). Consider a stop at the Museum of Anthropology or a stroll through the Nitobe Memorial Garden along the way.

6 Arbutus Greenway

DISTANCE:	8.7 km (5.4 miles) one-way
ELEVATION GAIN:	Up to 122 m (400 feet)
HIGH POINT:	76 m (250 feet)
DIFFICULTY:	Easy
FITNESS:	Walkers, runners, bicyclists
FAMILY-FRIENDLY:	Yes, and wheelchair- and jogging stroller–friendly
DOG-FRIENDLY:	On leash
AMENITIES:	Benches, interpretive signs, washrooms
CONTACT/MAPS:	City of Vancouver Department of Streets and Transportation
BEFORE YOU GO:	Limited or restricted parking at both terminuses. Best (and free) parking options on neighborhood streets around Quilchena Park.
GPS:	N49.242 W123.147

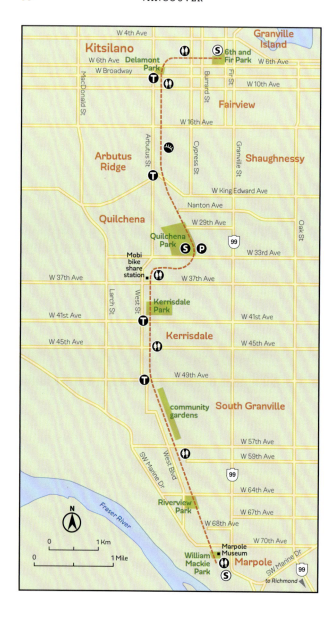

Granville
Island

Kitsilano

W 4th Ave

W 6th Ave   Delamont
Park

S 6th and
   Fir Park

W 6th Ave

Fir St

W Broadway

W 10th Ave

MacDonald St

Burrard St

Fairview

W 16th Ave

Cypress St

Granville St

Shaughnessy

Arbutus
Ridge

Arbutus St

W King Edward Ave

Quilchena

Nanton Ave

W 29th Ave

Oak St

Quilchena
Park

S P

99

W 33rd Ave

Mobi
bike
share
station

W 37th Ave

West St

W 37th Ave

Larch St

Kerrsdale
Park

W 41st Ave

W 41st Ave

W 45th Ave

Kerrisdale

W 45th Ave

W 49th Ave

community
gardens

South Granville

SW Marine Dr

West Blvd

W 57th Ave

W 59th Ave

99

W 64th Ave

Riverview
Park

Fraser River

W 67th Ave

W 68th Ave

W 70th Ave

N

0   1 Km

0   1 Mile

William
Mackie
Park

Marpole
Museum

Marpole

S

SW Marine Dr

99

to Richmond

GETTING THERE

Map to: Quilchena Park, Vancouver, BC. **Transit:**TransLink buses 4, 7, 14, 50, 84 on W. 4th Avenue and Fir Street near northern terminus; 99 on W. Broadway; 16 on W. 12th Avenue, West Boulevard, W. 64th Avenue, and Arbutus Street; 25 on W. King Edward Avenue; R4 and 41 on W. 41st Avenue; 49 on W. 49th Avenue; 10 on SW Marine Drive near southern terminus. **Parking:** Park on neighborhood streets.

Walk, run, or bike from the Fraser River to False Creek on this wonderful, paved 8.7-km (5.4-mile) rail trail. The Arbutus Greenway follows a section of an old light-rail line, once dubbed "The Sockeye Special" because it transported workers to the thriving cannery community of Steveston on Lulu Island. Explore the greenway, traveling through leafy residential areas and vibrant commercial centers. Skirt treed parks, pass historical structures, and admire processions of community gardens. Along the way, enjoy a few good views of North Shore summits.

GET MOVING

After the last train used this corridor in 2001, Canadian Pacific Railway (CPR)—which owned the railway—wanted to develop it. The City of Vancouver wanted to transform it into a travel corridor and greenbelt. The Supreme Court of British Columbia ruled in favor of CPR, but ultimately the railroad sold the corridor to the city in 2016, which then transformed it into the Arbutus Greenway. The city plans to add a streetcar line paralleling the wide, paved bike-pedestrian path.

The greenway is named after Arbutus Street, a major arterial that parallels it for a good stretch. Arbutuses are known as madronas in Washington and Oregon and madrones in California. They favor dry coastal areas like the Gulf Islands, but pockets can be found in the Lower Mainland.

The Greenway is heavily used by commuting cyclists, but plenty of folks also use it for short walks and long runs. From Quilchena Park, an out-and-back in either direction makes for a good outing. By catching a bus on Arbutus Street, you can plan for a one-way trip. Below is a brief description of the greenway from south to north.

The Greenway starts near the North Arm Fraser River, on Milton Street just west of SW Marine Drive in Marpole, one

Community gardens line long stretches of the Greenway.

of Vancouver's oldest neighborhoods. It then slowly ascends, passing William Mackie Park, which houses the Marpole Museum in the historic 1912-built Colbourne House. At 0.5 km (0.3 mile), cross SW Marine Drive and continue, slowly ascending through quiet neighborhoods and along Riverview Park.

At 1.1 km (0.7 mile) cross W. 64th Avenue. The way slowly but steadily gains elevation, crossing W. 57th Avenue at 1.9 km (1.2 miles) with its original railroad signals. The trail then passes a large strip of well-tended and attractive community gardens before entering the bustling commercial district of the historic Kerrisdale neighborhood. At 3.7 km (2.3 miles), cross busy W. 41st Avenue, where plenty of cafés and eateries beckon you to take a break.

On a now-level grade, pass the Kerrisdale Arena, where Bill Haley and the Comets performed at the city's first rock concert in 1956. At the W. 37th Avenue crossing, look for the Mobi bike share station if you're interested in switching your mode of travel.

The trail begins to descend, bending east before curving northwest, straddling the tony Arbutus Ridge and Shaughnessy neighborhoods. Pass beautiful homes along leafy streets and viewpoints of North Shore peaks, including the iconic twin summits called The Lions (Two Sisters). At 5 km (3.1 miles), cross W. 33rd Avenue and come to Quilchena Park with its trails, large trees, lawns, and washrooms. The trail continues descending, crossing W. King Edward Avenue at 6.2 km (3.9 miles).

Continuing northward into the Kitsilano neighborhood, the landscape becomes more urbanized upon crossing W. 16th Avenue. At 7.6 km (4.7 miles), come to W. Broadway, where a detour is currently in place until the overpass is finalized. A stop on the new SkyTrain Millennium Line extension is slated to open here in 2025, connecting the Greenway to Vancouver's wonderful light rail system.

The trail continues, passing city blocks before bending eastward into the Fairview neighborhood and passing another large community garden complex. Cross Cypress Street, a designated bike route for connecting to the Seawall and Burrard Street Bridge. One block farther, cross busy Burrard Street. Then pass a pocket park before reaching the trail's northern terminus at Fir Street, 8.7 km (5.4 miles) from the start. From here, you can reach the Seawall (Trail 2) by following city streets north for about 0.6 km (0.4 mile).

THE LIONS (TWO SISTERS): VANCOUVER'S ICONIC PEAKS

The Lions are among the most recognizable spires of the North Shore Mountains, which form the backdrop of the Vancouver metropolitan area. Former premier of the colony of New Brunswick and one of the Fathers of Confederation, John Hamilton Gray bestowed the name "The Lions" on the twin summits during his tenure in Vancouver as a justice of the Supreme Court of British Columbia. He thought the peaks looked like lions couchant from heraldry.

To the Squamish First Nation, on whose ancestral lands the lions lay, these impressive, pointed peaks were known as Ch'ích'iyúy Elxwíḵn, the Two Sisters (or Twin Sisters). And according to one of their legends, the Sisters were responsible for bringing the warring Squamish and Haida peoples together in peace. The two peaks, West Lion (elev. 1646 m/5400 feet) and East Lion (elev. 1606 m/5269 feet) can be seen from throughout Vancouver, Burnaby, Richmond, and Surrey, lending their name to such features and entities as the Lions Gate Bridge, BC Lions (Canadian Football League), Lions Gate Entertainment, Lions Gate Fisheries, and Granville Island Brewing's Lions Winter Ale among them.

While the summits are technical climbs and lie within the Capilano watershed (which is officially closed to the public), they can be viewed from near their summit bases on the Howe Sound Crest Trail (outside the scope of this book). Excellent, fairly close views can also be had from trails in Cypress Provincial Park (see Trails 18 and 19) and Capilano River Regional Park (Trail 21).

7 VanDusen Botanical Garden

DISTANCE:	More than 7 km (4.3 miles) of trails
ELEVATION GAIN:	Up to 40 m (130 feet)
HIGH POINT:	115 m (380 feet)
DIFFICULTY:	Easy
FITNESS:	Walkers
FAMILY-FRIENDLY:	Yes, and some trails wheelchair- and jogging stroller–friendly
DOG-FRIENDLY:	Prohibited, except service dogs
AMENITIES:	Water, washrooms, benches, interpretive signs, restaurant, café, library, visitor center, gift shop
CONTACT/MAPS:	City of Vancouver Parks, Recreation, and Cultural Services
BEFORE YOU GO:	Open year-round, except Christmas. Hours vary throughout the year; consult website. Admission fee; purchase tickets on-site or online.
GPS:	N49.238 W123.130

GETTING THERE

Map to: VanDusen Parking, Vancouver, BC. **Transit:** TransLink buses 17; 10 on Granville Avenue; R4 and 41 on W. 41st Avenue. **Parking:** Free parking lot for the botanical garden, but it can fill on weekends. Abundant free street parking along W. 37th Avenue. Electric vehicle charging stations in parking area.

Wander through manicured gardens, forested groves, and rolling meadows. Saunter along placid ponds and a cascading creek. And admire sculptures and totem poles among more than 7500 species of plants from throughout the world. You can walk for kilometers on trails of varying designs through this magnificent 22-ha (55-acre) botanical garden and still not see it all. All the better for return trips—each season brings its own magic.

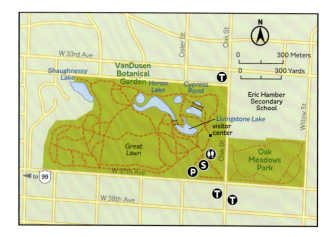

GET MOVING

Transformed from an old golf course in the tony Shaughnessy neighborhood, the VanDusen Botanical Garden is one of the crown jewels of Vancouver's park system. Its name honors lumberman and philanthropist Whitford Julian VanDusen, who helped establish the Vancouver Foundation, one of the largest community foundations in the country. The gardens are jointly managed by the Vancouver Park Board and the Vancouver Botanical Gardens Association (VBGA), who oversee a dedicated staff and nearly a thousand volunteers. The grounds are impeccably cared for and maintained.

From the visitor center (which is LEED Platinum–certified), open the door and be greeted by Livingstone Lake—and more than likely, a throng of selfie warriors with perhaps a few professional photographers as well. These grounds are a favorite for capturing images and special moments like weddings. From the lake, you have lots of trail options, so just set off and enjoy the floral show. Explore the bodies of water with their aquatic plants. Walk across Cypress Pond on a floating bridge.

Floral collections and gardens at VanDusen include the Canadian Heritage Garden, where you can walk through all of Canada's forest zones. Check out the Sino-Himalayan plants, Japanese maples, cherry groves, rose gardens, Mediterranean Garden, giant sequoias, heather garden, South African Garden, Chilean Garden, ginkgoes, and Australian and New Zealand Garden.

Visit in late spring and be blown away on the Rhododendron Walk, with its nearly one thousand varieties of rhodies. Come in the fall and follow the Autumn Stroll through the Eastern North America area, where you will be dazzled by the brilliant colors of eastern hardwoods. The garden issues a monthly bloom guide of what's in season. And any season

Giant wooden owl in VanDusen's BC Habitat Garden

is a good time to let the kids burn some energy in the maze. Afterward, savor a few minutes in the Meditation Garden. You can easily walk 5 to 7 km (3.1 to 4.3 miles) in VanDusen. A walk just around the periphery is about 3 km (1.9 miles).

GO FARTHER

Combine this walk with nearby Queen Elizabeth Park (Trail 8), easily reached by walking 1.3 km (0.8 mile) from VanDusen. Cross Oak Street and walk northeast through Oak Meadows Park. Then walk north on Willow Street before turning east on W. 33rd Avenue to reach Queen Elizabeth Park.

8 Queen Elizabeth Park

DISTANCE:	More than 5 km (3.1 miles) of trails
ELEVATION GAIN:	Up to 90 m (300 feet)
HIGH POINT:	125 m (410 feet)
DIFFICULTY:	Easy to moderate
FITNESS:	Walkers, runners
FAMILY-FRIENDLY:	Yes, and several trails wheelchair- and jogging stroller–friendly
DOG-FRIENDLY:	On leash, plus separate off-leash area
AMENITIES:	Water, washrooms, benches, picnic tables, interpretive signs, restaurant, sports fields and courts, public art, arboretum, Bloedel Conservatory
CONTACT/MAPS:	City of Vancouver Parks, Recreation, and Cultural Services
GPS:	N49.241 W123.115

GETTING THERE

Map to: Queen Elizabeth Park, Vancouver, BC. **Transit:** TransLink buses 15, 33; SkyTrain Canada Line via King Edward or Oakridge-41st Avenue Stations. **Parking:** Paid parking at Queen Elizabeth Park; additional paid parking available at Sunrise Spot near Bloedel Conservatory entrance.

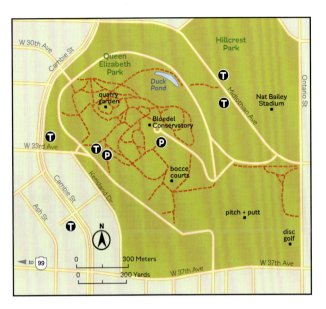

Enjoy sweeping views of the city from this small but delightful park located on Little Mountain, the highest point in Vancouver. Stroll through gardens in old quarries and past delightful sculptures. Come for sunrises and sunsets and when the park's cherry blossoms, rhododendrons, and roses are in bloom. And if you need a good workout, trails heading up and down this hilltop park will give you a good cardio boost.

GET MOVING

It's hard to imagine that this ornately landscaped and manicured 52-ha (128-acre) park was once an open hilltop reservoir with two quarries, which were used to build early city roads. The quarries are now beautifully landscaped gardens, the larger one complete with a waterfall and small pond. The reservoir has been capped and transformed into a hilltop plaza with benches, sculptures, fountains, and the geodesic dome (the first in Canada) of the Bloedel Conservatory.

The park was dedicated to King George VI and his consort, Queen Elizabeth (mother of Queen Elizabeth II), during their 1939 visit to the city. Soon afterward, the northern part of the park became Canada's first civic arboretum, containing trees from across Canada as well as many exotic species. The park is exceptionally beautiful during spring blossoming and autumn foliage.

Queen Elizabeth Park is also known for its sculptures, including *Knife Edge Two Piece* by renowned British sculptor

The "subjects" in the park's popular Photo Session sculpture

Henry Moore, and *Photo Session* by J. Seward Johnson Jr. The latter is a bronze sculpture of a man photographing three people and always has a line of visitors joining the session for their own photos. And wedding photographers are everywhere in the park, as it's one of the most popular places in the city to tie the knot.

Most of the trails are paved and short, but a few dirt and longer trails traverse the northern part of the park—past big trees, across lawns, and along the Duck Pond. Enjoy people-watching as you explore the park, passing a bocce ball court, disc golf course, and pitch and putt course. The park borders Hillcrest Park with its Nat Bailey Stadium. Named for baseball promoter and founder of the White Spot restaurant chain, "The Nat" can be a lively place when the Vancouver Canadians, a Minor League Baseball team, is playing.

A hike or run around the park is about 3 km (1.9 miles), while a trip around the quarry gardens is around 1.3 km (0.8 mile). You can easily do a 5-km (3.1-mile) run through the park with little trail repeating, Do plan on lounging on the hilltop plaza, taking in sweeping views of the city, North Shore peaks, San Juan and Gulf Islands, and Mount Baker. And consider a visit inside the Bloedel Conservatory (fee). Within its dome are more than a hundred species of tropical rainforest and desert birds, exotic fish, and five hundred species of exotic plants.

GO FARTHER

A 1-km (0.6-mile) walk east on W. 37th Avenue will deliver you to the 43-ha (106-acre) Mountain View Cemetery, jokingly referred to as the dead center of Vancouver. It actually is the geographic center of Vancouver and, true to its name, has mountain views. It also has lots of history and makes for a good, contemplative walk.

Next page: Central Park's Lower Pond (Trail 12)

BURNABY & NEW WESTMINSTER

From the Fraser River to Burrard Inlet, the city of Burnaby's land was once populated by villages of Halkomelem- and Squamish-speaking Coast Salish First Nations. Today, it is the province's third-largest city (population 300,000) and home to Simon Fraser University and BC Institute of Technology. Parks and greenbelts make up a quarter of its land mass—one of the highest percentages of any North American city.

The city of Burnaby was named after Robert Burnaby, who was private secretary to Richard Clement Moody, British Columbia's founder and first lieutenant governor. Moody also founded the city of New Westminster (population 90,000), establishing it as the capital of the new colony in 1859. New Westminster remained the capital until 1866, when the colonies of British Columbia and Vancouver Island merged and Victoria became the new capital.

New Westminster's name was bestowed by Queen Victoria, after the city's proposed name of Queensborough (now a neighborhood) received a tepid response from London. The second most densely populated city in Canada (behind Vancouver), it's been experiencing explosive growth. Colloquially referred to as New West, the city boasts many historic buildings and neighborhoods, as well as the oldest public park in the province. And the downtown waterfront has been undergoing redevelopment, bringing with it new parks and trails along the Fraser River.

9

Burnaby Mountain Conservation Area

DISTANCE:	More than 31 km (19 miles) of trails
ELEVATION GAIN:	Up to 325 m (1065 feet)
HIGH POINT:	350 m (1150 feet)
DIFFICULTY:	Easy to difficult
FITNESS:	Walkers, runners, hikers, bicyclists
FAMILY-FRIENDLY:	Yes
DOG-FRIENDLY:	On leash
AMENITIES:	Washrooms, water, benches, interpretive signs, sculptures, playground, concessions
CONTACT/MAPS:	City of Burnaby Parks, Recreation, and Culture
BEFORE YOU GO:	Open dawn to dusk
GPS:	N49.288 W122.925

GETTING THERE

Map to: Mountain Air Bike Skills Park, Port Moody, BC. **Transit:** TransLink buses R5, 143, 144, 145, 160. **Parking:** Large parking area off Barnet Highway on conservation area's north side. Alternative parking can be found on the south side of the conservation area along Gaglardi Way and at a lot near the summit off Centennial Way.

Home to Simon Fraser University, 370-meter (1214-foot) Burnaby Mountain also contains a sprawling 576-ha (1423-acre) conservation area that completely encircles the mountaintop campus. Take to its large trail network for an easy summit stroll or for a vigorous climb up and over this Metro Vancouver landmark. Dillydally on the summit, enjoying sculptures, gardens, or a picnic on an inviting lawn. And take in splendid views of the Vancouver skyline, Burrard Inlet below, and a backdrop of rugged North Shore summits.

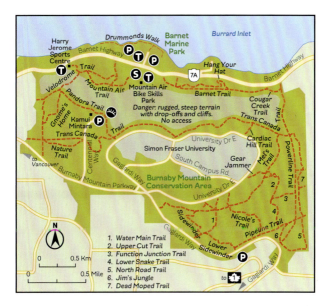

1. Water Main Trail
2. Upper Cut Trail
3. Function Junction Trail
4. Lower Snake Trail
5. North Road Trail
6. Jim's Jungle
7. Dead Moped Trail

GET MOVING

From the trailhead, you can only go east or west along the base of the mountain. The northern face of Burnaby Mountain has cliffs and is extremely steep, so it's closed to the public. However, two trails ascend the mountain from the north at the conservation area's eastern and western ends. Both trails will get your heart rate up, especially the Velodrome Trail with its five hundred steps. This trail is closed to bikes, one of just a few on the mountain. Mountain biking is popular here, especially in the south end of the conservation area.

For an excellent loop hike, leave the trailhead on the well-graded Mountain Air Trail, waking west through a forest of mature hemlocks and cedars. At 1.4 km (0.9 mile), come to a junction where a trail descends right to the Harry Jerome Sports Centre (named for North Vancouver's Afro Canadian track and field standout, Olympic medal winner, and Canada Sports Hall of Famer).

A young hiker tackles the Velodrome Trail's 500 steps.

Turn left here on the Velodrome Trail and work those steps! At 2.1 km (1.3 miles), catch your breath and head left on the Pandora Trail, ascending more moderately through open lawns and passing the mountain's notable attractions. The Kamui Mintara is particularly striking: Japanese for "Playground of the Gods," it includes wooden sculptures by Ainu (Aboriginal Japanese) sculptor Nuburi Toko and his son, Shusei Toko, commemorating the goodwill between Burnaby and its sister city, Kushiro, on Japan's Hokkaido Island.

The trail continues past excellent viewpoints (especially of Burrard Inlet to the north), a restaurant, rose garden, and playground. This area is also easily accessible by road from the south. At 3.4 km (2.1 miles), reach the Trans Canada Trail. Take it left through quiet forest just below the mountain's broad summit and above its steep northern slopes. A couple of trails, including the Cardiac Hill Trail, lead right to the mountaintop Simon Fraser University. Established in 1965 as Fraser University, the name was quickly changed to Simon Fraser University because the school's original initials, FU, had a profane meaning. The public university, however, is highly ranked and has one heck of a gorgeous setting.

After a slow descent, reach a junction at 6.4 km (4 miles) with the Powerline Trail. Turn left here, continuing on the Trans Canada Trail and steeply descending to the Cougar Creek Trail at 7.2 km (4.5 miles). Turn left and follow it to the Barnet Trail, continuing along a powerline and returning to your start at 9.3 km (5.8 miles).

Consider exploring some of the mountain's southern trails too, with lots of loop options available. The trails on the mountain's western slopes also allow for some easy to moderate loops and can be combined with the Trans Canada Trail.

GO FARTHER

From the Barnet Road trailhead, you can walk (or drive and park) to Barnet Marine Park. Cross a set of railroad tracks on a large bridge and then follow the lovely, wide, and wheelchair-accessible Drummonds Walk, which spans 1.6 km (1 mile). This trail travels along the shores of Burrard Inlet, granting sweeping views of the waterway. Watch for a myriad of birds, and check out several historical sites, including First Nations harvesting areas, an old pier, and the ruins of an old logging mill and camp. At one point, the Barnet Mill was the largest lumber mill in the British Empire, employing large numbers of Chinese, Japanese, and East Indian laborers.

10 Burnaby Lake Regional Park

DISTANCE:	More than 19 km (12 miles) of trails
ELEVATION GAIN:	Up to 75 m (250 feet)
HIGH POINT:	30 m (100 feet)
DIFFICULTY:	Easy
FITNESS:	Walkers, runners, hikers
FAMILY-FRIENDLY:	Yes, and several trails wheelchair- and jogging stroller–friendly
DOG-FRIENDLY:	On leash
AMENITIES:	Water, washrooms, benches, interpretive signs, observation tower, picnic area, Nature House
CONTACT/MAPS:	Metro Vancouver Regional Parks
BEFORE YOU GO:	Bikes are not allowed on trails. Several kilometers of horse-riding trails.
GPS:	N49.246 W122.919

GETTING THERE

Map to: Burnaby Horsemen's Association, Burnaby, BC. **Transit:** TransLink buses 101, 110, 136, 144; SkyTrain Millenium Line stops at Production Way-University Station. **Parking:** Park at the Avalon Avenue trailhead near the equestrian center. Alternative parking lots can be found on Glencarin Drive and Piper Avenue.

Aside from the noise of zooming cars on the Trans-Canada Highway and clanking trains on the railway, you'd be hard-pressed to feel like you're in the heart of British Columbia's third-largest city while hiking at Burnaby Lake. The regional park encompasses nearly the entire 312-ha (770-acre) lake. Once lined with sawmills and badly polluted by the 1960s, the lake has since been cleaned up and is now one of the best birding spots in Burnaby. Hikers, runners, and walkers of all ages and abilities can be seen here year-round, following the well-groomed and near-level trails around the lake.

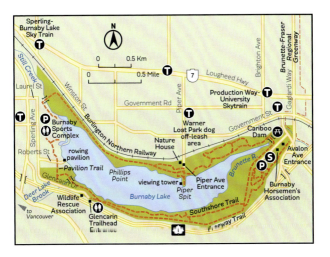

GET MOVING

Wedged between the Trans-Canada Highway and a Canadian National Railway line, Burnaby Lake is situated in a busy travel corridor. But the large park is part of a greenway, forming a green swath home to copious critters (including the occasional bear) within the corridor. The lake is popular with rowers and houses a rowing pavilion. The park is also popular with equestrians, with an equestrian center and a network of horse trails.

Most hikers, runners, and walkers take to the Avalon, Southshore, Pavilion, Cottonwood, and Brunette Headwaters Trails—when combined, they form the 10.3-km (6.4-mile) Burnaby Lake Loop (signed with a Canada Goose) around the lake. This loop offers varied sights and opportunities to expand your trip by adding on side trails. Starting the loop from the Avalon trailhead near the Burnaby Horsemen's Association head west, traversing an attractive forest of cedars, hemlocks, and spruce before approaching the Glencarin trailhead. The 2.7-km (1.7-mile) Freeway Trail runs parallel to the loop here, offering a shorter loop option if you're ready to return to your start.

The Burnaby Lake Loop continues west past the Wildlife Rescue Association of BC compound and then emerges
on boardwalks, passing by birches and traversing the lake's
grassy shoreline. The lake was formed by a glacier twelve
thousand years ago. Since urbanization around it began

Crossing the bridge over Deer Lake Brook

in the late 1800s, the lake has been affected by heavy silting, resulting in much of its surface area becoming marshy. Enjoy good views across the lake to Burnaby Mountain. On a big bridge, cross a brook flowing out from nearby Deer Lake (Trail 11) and then head north, passing the rowing pavilion and skirting the large Burnaby Sports Complex.

The loop then crosses Still Creek on a bridge and bends east along the north shore, paralleling railroad tracks. Traverse large cottonwood groves and pass the short spur to Phillips Point, offering good views across the lake. The loop then reaches the busy Piper Spit area near the Piper Avenue Entrance. Here you have the opportunity to hike a couple of small loops, visit the Nature House (hours limited), check out the observation tower with its expanded views of the lake, or take the small spur out to Piper Spit. This is a birding hot spot, with mallards, teals, wood ducks, Canada geese, scaups, and pintails in profuse numbers.

The loop then continues east through attractive forest, passing the short Conifer and Spruce Loop Trails before reaching the Cariboo Dam on the Brunette River, the lake's outlet. Here a trail leads left connecting to the Brunette-Fraser Regional Greenway. The lake loop leads right, crossing the dam and then shortly afterward returning to the Avalon Avenue trailhead.

GO FARTHER

You can extend your wandering by following the Brunette-Fraser Regional Greenway along the Brunette River for 2.1 km (1.3 miles) to Hume Park. There are also several kilometers of trails in adjacent Robert Burnaby Park, but no pedestrian access from Burnaby Lake Park because of the Trans-Canada Highway separating the parks.

11   Deer Lake

DISTANCE:	More than 12 km (7.5 miles) of trails
ELEVATION GAIN:	Up to 85 m (280 feet)
HIGH POINT:	105 m (345 feet)
DIFFICULTY:	Easy
FITNESS:	Walkers, runners, hikers
FAMILY-FRIENDLY:	Yes, and many trails wheelchair- and jogging–stroller friendly
DOG-FRIENDLY:	On leash
AMENITIES:	Washrooms, benches, picnic tables, interpretive signs, beach, boat launch
CONTACT/MAPS:	City of Burnaby Parks, Recreation, and Culture
BEFORE YOU GO:	Open from dawn to dusk
GPS:	N49.236 W122.965

GETTING THERE

Map to: Deer Lake Park, Sperling Avenue, Burnaby, BC. **Transit:** TransLink buses 110, 123, 144. **Parking:** Park in the main lot off Sperling Avenue. Alternative parking areas at the Burnaby Art Gallery, Century Gardens, and Shadbolt Centre for the Arts on Deer Lake Avenue, and off Royal Oak Avenue.

Burnaby's crown jewel park, Deer Lake sits in the city's center surrounded by meadows, towering cottonwoods, and gorgeously preserved Edwardian country homes. Part of the city's cultural center, Deer Lake Park is also home to the Burnaby Art Gallery, Shadbolt Centre for the Arts, Burnaby Village Museum, and some beautiful gardens. Roam the park's well-maintained trails and boardwalks, marveling at its pastoral landscape while looking out at North Shore Mountains and Metrotown skyscrapers.

GET MOVING

Deer Lake Park is a well-loved park, not just for its location near municipal offices and its wonderful trail system, but also

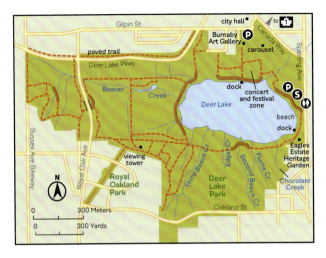

for its aesthetics. Deer Lake's meadows, manicured lawns, and historical, stately country homes give it an Eastern Canadian or European feeling. But when you wander on the park's upper slopes, looking out over the lake at a fortress of imposing mountains, there's no doubt you're in British Columbia.

From the Sperling Avenue parking lot, set out on the Deer Lake Loop, a popular and scenic 3.4-km (2.1-mile) journey around the lovely lake, most of it on boardwalk. If it's summer, your start will be packed with folks wading at the lake's beach or launching a kayak, canoe, or paddleboard. The loop makes bridged crossings of several creeks, as well as traverses a long stretch of marshy meadow on the lake's western shores. The landscape is pastoral and quite a contrast to the row of high-rises perched on a ridge in the background. Near the trailhead, visit the beautiful 1929-built Eagles Estate Heritage Garden.

To the west of the lake, you can extend your lake loop with a 2.4-km (1.5-mile) loop around the marshy meadows. The northern leg is particularly pleasing, traveling along Angelo and Beaver Creeks and a row of towering cottonwoods. At the western end of the loop, south of the Royal Oak Avenue trailhead, you can follow a trail under a bridge on Royal Oak Avenue and hike a hilly kilometer (0.6 mile) of trail through a quiet forest. You can return on paved paths paralleling Sussex Avenue, Deer Lake Parkway, and Royal Oak Avenue.

Several trails lead south from the loop, climbing an open hillside. There is a small viewing tower, but better views of the lake are from the trails to its east. Here you'll notice some ruins of structures that were all once part of a prison farm. For more on that—and an excellent workout—head up the 0.6-km (0.4-mile) linear trail through Royal Oakland Park. This trail is basically an elaborate stairway with 312 steps delivering you to Oakland Street, close to a slew of excellent Asian eateries on the Kingsway in Burnaby's Metrotown. At

Metrotown skyscrapers form a contrasting background to tranquil Deer Lake.

Royal Oakland Park, the trail uses the original front stairway of the notorious Oakalla Prison, which operated from 1912 until 1991 and was the site of several executions. The area has since been redeveloped into charming condos, with the farmlands now part of the park. But those steps give off a chilling aura.

On a much more upbeat note, be sure to check out the trails leading north from the lake loop through the park's cultural center. Check out the art gallery and center, museum, carousel, and the beautiful Century Gardens with its rhododendrons. Admire, too, the sprawling Edwardian country homes that were built here in the early part of the twentieth century, when Burnaby was still a pretty rural community. Well-to-do Vancouver and New Westminster businesspeople built their estates to replicate the English countryside. Download an interpretive brochure and take the Heritage Walk.

12 Central Park

DISTANCE:	More than 12 km (7.5 miles) of trails
ELEVATION GAIN:	Up to 45 m (150 feet)
HIGH POINT:	130 m (430 feet)
DIFFICULTY:	Easy
FITNESS:	Walkers, runners
FAMILY-FRIENDLY:	Yes, and most trails wheelchair- and jogging stroller-friendly
DOG-FRIENDLY:	On leash
AMENITIES:	Water, washrooms, benches, picnic tables, interpretive signs, concessions, sports fields and courts, public art, pool, pitch and putt golf course
CONTACT/MAPS:	City of Burnaby Parks, Recreation, and Culture
BEFORE YOU GO:	Open from dawn to dusk; electric vehicle charging stations available
GPS:	N49.232 W123.0200

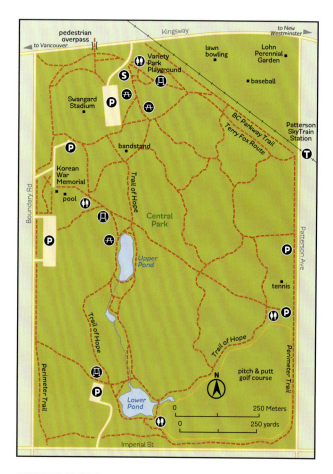

GETTING THERE

Map to: Central Park Picnic Areas, Burnaby, BC. **Transit:** TransLink buses 19, 31, 49, 110, 129; SkyTrain Expo Line stops at Patterson Station. **Parking:** Free parking available at Central Park's main lot off Kingsway; other options can be found in parking lots off Boundary Road, Patterson Avenue, and Imperial Street.

Located in Burnaby's bustling Metrotown along its boundary with Vancouver, Central Park is a green oasis surrounded by concrete and glass. A former military outpost, Central Park packs a lot within its 86.4 ha (213 acres). Wander on kilometers of wide, well-built trails through groves of towering conifers to two small ponds. And admire gardens, historical structures, memorials, and sculptures along the way.

GET MOVING

Central Park was initially established as a military reserve along the False Creek Trail (now Kingsway) between Vancouver and New Westminster, created to defend New West (then BC's capital city) from an American attack—an assault that never occurred. In 1891, one year before Burnaby became incorporated, the reserve became a park. Today, it's a classic city park bustling with sports activities, playing children, and lots of runners and walkers.

Vancouver's second mayor, David Oppenheimer, named the park after *the* Central Park for his New York–raised wife—as well as for its central location on the British Columbia Electric Railway's (BCER) Vancouver–New Westminster interurban line. Oppenheimer helped establish the BCER. Prior to the park's establishment, the Royal Naval Reserves logged the old growth here to use as masts. But the replacing second-growth forest is now quite mature, tall, and impressive.

You can walk willy-nilly through the park, enjoying its many facets. Or you can take one of its three marked routes. The 2.5-km (1.6-mile) Trail of Hope (named for Terry Fox's Marathon of Hope; see sidebar) starts near the picnic area, traverses lovely forest, and travels by the Upper and Lower Ponds, both teeming with waterfowl. The 5-km (3.1-mile) Terry Fox Route sweeps by the ponds, leads through the forest, and swings by the stadium and picnic areas on the paved BC Parkway Trail. This route also hosts Burnaby's annual Terry

Fox Run, a fundraiser for cancer research. The Perimeter Trail travels 3.5 km (2.2 miles) around the park's edges on a soft, rubberized surface and is fully lit. It's perfect for giving your knees a break and getting outside during winter's gloom and early darkness.

Along the periphery, stop to admire the impressive Korean War Memorial's *Ambassador of Peace* sculpture. And locate the plaque commemorating the Prince (Now King Charles) and Princess of Wales's dedication of the park's Variety Park Playground. You'll have plenty of docile black squirrels to accompany you throughout the park.

Towering trees shade a placid path in this former military reserve.

TERRY FOX AND THE MARATHON OF HOPE

Port Coquitlam resident Terrance Stanley Fox touched an entire nation with his courage, inspiration, and determination. At eighteen years old, Terry lost his right leg to osteogenic sarcoma. After going through sixteen months of treatment and seeing people suffer in the cancer wards, he was determined to raise money for cancer research. He decided to do it by running across Canada in a Marathon of Hope, in an effort to raise $24 million, one dollar for each Canadian at the time.

On April 12, 1980, twenty-two-year old Terry—now fitted with a prosthetic leg—left Newfoundland and Labrador to begin his run across Canada. He began without much notice, but by the time he entered Ontario, he had become a national sensation. He was met by politicians including Prime Minster Pierre Trudeau, sports celebrities like Bobby Orr, and business leaders. He drew the attention of Isadore Sharp, founder and CEO of Four Seasons Hotels, who lost a son to melanoma a year after Terry's diagnosis. Sharp persuaded almost one thousand other corporations to pledge donations.

Terry ran for 143 days, covering 5373 km (3339 miles)—the equivalent of a marathon (42.2 km/26.2 miles) a day—before having to stop just shy of Thunder Bay, Ontario, on September 1. By that time, his bone cancer had metastasized to his lungs. He passed away the following year on June 28, 1981, just shy of his twenty-third birthday. Today his Marathon of Hope continues to inspire people worldwide.

Fox was posthumously awarded many honors, including the youngest person ever honored as a Companion of the Order of Canada. Schools were named after him, including the Port Coquitlam high school from which he graduated, as well as buildings, cancer-research units, trails, and even a mountain.

Outside of BC Place in downtown Vancouver is a series of four bronze sculptures depicting Fox running, designed by Douglas Coupland. And Fox's hometown of Port Coquitlam recently unveiled the Terry Fox Hometown Square, a plaza with installations about the Marathon of Hope.

During Fox's marathon, Sharp proposed the annual Terry Fox Runs which have grown to involve millions of participants in more than sixty countries and have raised more than $850 million for cancer research. Visit the Terry Fox Foundation (terryfox.org) for more about Terry, the Terry Fox Runs, and the Terry Fox Research Institution.

GO FARTHER

The paved BC Parkway Trail traverses the park. You can follow this 18-km (11.2-mile) path (with some road sections) west to Trout Lake Park (John Hendry Park) in Vancouver, or east to Quayside Park on the Fraser River in New Westminster. It primarily follows the SkyTrain, which mostly uses the original BCER interurban line corridor. It's popular with bike commuters. Run or walk it one-way and return via the SkyTrain.

13 | Fraser Foreshore Trail

DISTANCE:	8 km (5 miles) one-way
ELEVATION GAIN:	Minimal
HIGH POINT:	6 m (20 feet)
DIFFICULTY:	Easy
FITNESS:	Walkers, runners, hikers, bicyclists
FAMILY-FRIENDLY:	Yes, and Burnaby section is wheelchair- and jogging stroller–friendly
DOG-FRIENDLY:	On leash; separate off-leash area and trail
AMENITIES:	Washrooms, benches, picnic tables and shelters, playgrounds, interpretive signs, lookout piers, volleyball courts
CONTACT/MAPS:	City of Burnaby Parks, Recreation, and Culture; City of Vancouver Parks, Recreation, and Cultural Services
BEFORE YOU GO:	Open from dawn to dusk
GPS:	N49.192 W122.999

GETTING THERE

Map to: Burnaby Fraser Foreshore Park, Burnaby, BC. **Transit:** TransLink bus 116 stops along N. Fraser Way; 100 stops along Marine Drive in Vancouver. **Parking:** Park in the lot at the corner of Byrne Road and Fraser Park Drive. Alternative parking along adjacent roads.

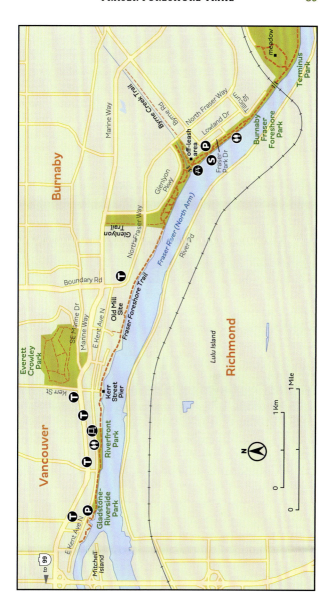

Walk or run along the Fraser River, the lifeline of the Lower Mainland. Traverse riparian forest, tidal mudflats, industrial complexes, a vibrant neighborhood redevelopment, and a string of delightful riverfront parks and greenbelts. Admire towering cottonwoods, perched eagles, plying tugboats, and sprawling log booms. And peer across the river to Lulu Island and its farms, contrasting nicely with the city vibe of Burnaby and Vancouver.

GET MOVING

The longest stretch of trail along the Fraser River in the Metro Vancouver Regional District, the Fraser Foreshore Trail travels from Burnaby's Big Bend neighborhood to Vancouver's Victoria-Fraserview neighborhood. It makes for a wonderful 16-km (10-mile) out-and-back bike ride, long run, or long walk—or you can sample smaller sections at a time.

From the Burnaby Fraser Foreshore Park parking lot, head west (downriver) or east (upriver). Heading eastward, the paved trail splits into two paralleling paths, traversing a green swath along the river interspersed with benches and exercise stations. At 0.6 km (0.4 mile), the parallel trails reunite at a large washroom. The way then continues along Fraser Park Drive. At 1.1 km (0.7 mile), it becomes dirt, ducks under a railroad bridge, and enters a large natural area referred to as Terminus Park. At 1.4 km (0.9 mile), come to a junction. The Foreshore Trail continues east through groves of giant cottonwoods along the river for another 0.5 km (0.3 mile), ending at a mudflat. Enjoy good views of log booms, puttering tugboats, and farms on Lulu Island—scenes more reminiscent of Vancouver's past than its burgeoning cosmopolitan present.

At the previous junction, you can also follow a 1-km (0.6-mile) loop around a small meadow, complete with barn owl nests. A short 0.2-km (0.1-mile) trail diverges north from it, crossing a slough and reaching Riverbend Drive.

Heading west from the Burnaby Fraser Foreshore Park parking lot, head downriver, crossing over a drainage canal and entering a picnic area. At 0.5 km (0.3 mile), cross Byrne Creek where two trails lead north along it on opposite creek

Boardwalk trail near Kerr Street Pier

beds. The Foreshore Trail splits in two and continues through a lovely greenbelt of riparian forest where eagles and osprey nest. The main paved path skirts Glenlyon Parkway, while the dirt path travels along the river shore. Connecting paths allow for loops.

At 1.4 km (0.9 mile), the Glenlyon Trail takes off north (heading 1.3 km/0.8 mile to Marine Way) at the junction where the paralleling dirt and paved paths of the Foreshore Trail reunite. Stay on the Foreshore Trail as it skirts an industrial center before reaching the Vancouver city line at Boundary Road at 2.4 km (1.5 miles). The trail then continues as a dirt path through former industrial lands undergoing a transition. For ninety years, this area was home to several massive wood-products mills. Now it is becoming a vibrant planned community known as the River District. Expect lots of changes here on return trips.

At 3.9 km (2.4 miles), reach the Kerr Street Pier, which calls out to be walked. The trail continues west through patches of riparian forest, passing residential areas and access points to roads and neighborhoods. At 4.5 km (2.8 miles), pass through the small Riverfront Park with a playground and washroom. The trail then skirts a company lot before traversing a greenbelt abutting quiet neighborhoods.

At 5.3 km (3.3 miles), pass through Gladstone-Riverside Park with its small pier. Then continue on pavement, skirting residences and small businesses and taking in views of industrial Mitchell Island before reaching the trail's end at 6.1 km (3.8 miles) on E. Kent Avenue N.

GO FARTHER

From the Kerr Street Pier, walk north on Kerr Street for 0.7 km (1.1 miles) to 38-ha (94-acre) Everett Crowley Park with its several kilometers of pleasant, forested trails.

14 Queen's and Glenbrook Ravine Parks

DISTANCE:	About 6 km (3.7 miles) of trails
ELEVATION GAIN:	Up to 85 m (280 feet)
HIGH POINT:	100 m (330 feet)
DIFFICULTY:	Easy
FITNESS:	Walkers, runners, hikers, bicyclists
FAMILY-FRIENDLY:	Yes, and Millennium Trail is wheelchair-accessible
DOG-FRIENDLY:	On leash; separate off-leash area
AMENITIES:	Washrooms, benches, picnic tables and shelters, playgrounds, sports field and courts, gardens
CONTACT/MAPS:	City of New Westminster Parks and Recreation
BEFORE YOU GO:	Queen's and Glenbrook Ravine Parks are not adjacent, requiring a short walk on city sidewalks.
GPS:	N49.213 W122.906

GETTING THERE

Map to: Queen's Park Rose Garden, New Westminster, BC.
Transit: TransLink buses 102, 105, 155; SkyTrain Expo Line stops at Columbia Station, requiring a 1-km (0.6-mile) walk via 4th Street, Royal Avenue, and Park Row. **Parking:** Along 3rd Avenue in Queen's Park and in lots located throughout the park.

The very first public park created in the colony of British Columbia, New Westminster's Queen's Park—like its host city—is rife with history. Explore manicured lawns, gardens, and big trees. Then head to Glenbrook Ravine Park for a wilder setting. Once the site of an old penitentiary and asylum, the ravine has since been restored to a more natural setting. Gravestones, memorials, and other traces of the institutions remain so that the dark histories of these places are not forgotten.

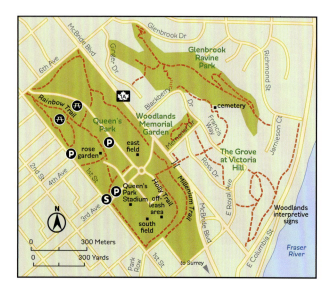

GET MOVING

Queen's Park was established in 1887 to celebrate Queen Victoria's jubilee year of reign. But the park's history goes back to 1859, when New Westminster was established as colonial British Columbia's capital city. "What a grand old Park this whole hill would make! I am reserving a very beautiful glen and adjoining ravine for the People and Park," wrote BC's first lieutenant governor, Richard Clement Moody, to BC Governor James Douglas.

Since its inception, Queen's Park has played a large role in the city's history—from constructing the province's first grand exhibition building, to training and housing combat and defense units during two World Wars; from welcoming Winston Churchill, King George VI, and Queen Elizabeth II, to being home to the professional lacrosse team, the Salmonbellies. And it's just a great park to take the kids, have a picnic, go for a jog, and enjoy a nice respite from the city.

Explore this classic city park by walking on the 2.5-km (1.6-mile) Millennium Trail, which travels along the 30-ha (75-acre) park's perimeter. Half soft-surfaced and half paved, it traverses rolling lawns and forest but also uses sidewalks along 1st Street. Skip the sidewalks by following the Rainbow Trail, passing the rose garden (splendid in spring) and a grove of some of the oldest Douglas-firs in New West. The park's Holly Trail swings through forest near the off-leash area.

After exploring Queens Park, walk northeast on sidewalks along E. Sixth Avenue to Glenbrook Drive, coming to

Rose Garden entrance in Queen's Park

the trailhead for Glenbrook Ravine in 0.4 km (0.25 mile). Now switchback down into the ravine, enjoying a quiet walk in the bustling city. The tree cover is primarily deciduous, as the original forest was logged long ago. Several side trails with stairs climb out of the ravine to neighborhood streets. The main ravine trail is a kilometer (0.6 mile) long, ending at a garden near a school on Jamieson Court.

For a return variation, take the side trail and steps up to Blackberry Drive, and then walk a short distance southeast

Queen's Park's Rainbow Trail

on a paved path to the old penitentiary cemetery. BC's first penitentiary stood across the ravine from 1872 to 1980. The grounds have since been redeveloped into townhouses. From the cemetery, continue on the paved path southeast and then curving northwest to Memorial Drive and the Woodlands Memorial Garden.

This emotion-invoking park contains more than five hundred grave markers set into memorial walls. Another wall lists all of the more than three thousand patients who died at Woodlands (BC's first large-scale mental health institution) and another nearby institution. The garden was built to honor the people who lived and died here, and to remind visitors to value all people.

You can return to Queen's Park via a pedestrian overpass on McBride Boulevard. A loop around Queen's Park including trails through the ravine and memorial garden is about 3.5 km (2.2 miles).

GO FARTHER

You can continue from the cemetery on paved paths through upscale condominium developments to pocket parks and several interpretive signs near the remnants of Woodlands. Or walk the old neighborhood streets west of Queen's Park. The 1865-built Irving House on Royal Avenue is the oldest home in the Lower Mainland that is still intact.

New Westminster has several inviting parks, trails, and promenades downtown along the Fraser River. From the Quayside off-leash dog park, walk 1.5 km (0.9 mile) on the Waterfront Esplanade to the Fraser River Discovery Centre. The Esplanade is under construction and will eventually continue another 0.7 km (0.4 mile) to Westminster Pier Park. You can also walk on another lovely, paved riverside path for 1 km (0.6 mile) through Sapperton Landing Park.

Next Page: Rice Lake in the Lower Seymour Conservation Reserve (Trail 25)

NORTH SHORE

West Vancouver (population 45,000) and the neighboring district and city of North Vancouver compose what is commonly referred to as the North Shore municipalities, or the North Shore. One of the wealthiest cities in Canada, West Vancouver (West Van) is set in a stunning location along English Bay at the base of the North Shore Mountains. The city boasts sprawling Cypress Provincial Park, with its excellent network of trails, stunning coastal parks, and a beautiful seawall trail.

North Vancouver (North Van) consists of two municipalities—the city of North Vancouver (population 65,000) and the district of North Vancouver (population 90,000). The district surrounds the city on three sides; it is much larger in area and population and is primarily residential. Laced with beautiful mountainous terrain and river valleys, North Van is home to several expansive regional and provincial parks, as well as one of the largest trail networks in the regional district.

Located in the mouth of Howe Sound and connected to West Vancouver's Horseshoe Bay by BC Ferries is lovely little Bowen Island. The ancestral hunting and fishing grounds of the Squamish people, today this island municipality (population 4200) consists primarily of retirees and commuters. In the early twentieth century, Bowen Island was a popular resort destination fueled by a steamship company. Crown lands and a regional district park on the island provide excellent hiking opportunities. Metro Parks is currently working on opening a new park, complete with camping and trails, at Cape Roger Curtis.

BOWEN ISLND

15 Crippen Regional Park

DISTANCE:	114 km (7.1 miles) of trails
ELEVATION GAIN:	Up to 110 m (360 feet)
HIGH POINT:	105 m (345 feet)
DIFFICULTY:	Easy to moderate
FITNESS:	Walkers, hikers, runners
FAMILY-FRIENDLY:	Yes, and many trails wheelchair-accessible
DOG-FRIENDLY:	Yes, on-leash and off-leash areas
AMENITIES:	Washrooms, interpretive signs, picnic tables and shelters
CONTACT/MAPS:	Metro Vancouver Regional Parks
BEFORE YOU GO:	Park open dawn to dusk; some trails open to equestrians
GPS:	N49.381 W123.334

GETTING THERE

Map to: Horseshoe Bay Ferry Terminal, West Vancouver, BC. **Transit:** TransLink buses 250, 257, 262 service Horseshoe Bay ferry terminal; 282 stops at Killarney Lake trailhead on Bowen Island. **Parking:** Park in Horseshoe Bay ferry terminal lot 1621 (fee) and walk onto the ferry for Snug Cove on Bowen Island. On Bowen Island walk 100 to 200 m (325 to 650 feet) to trailheads.

Wander on old carriage roads and well-built trails, traversing lovely island landscapes that once hosted thousands of steamship-arriving vacationers from the Lower Mainland and beyond. Travel through groves of mature conifers and wildlife-rich wetlands. Amble around a placid lake and alongside a tumbling creek. And explore tidal flats, a coastal bluff, and a handful of historical structures harkening back to the island's early days of non-Native settlement.

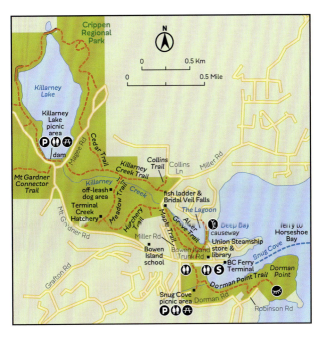

GET MOVING

From the ferry terminal, walk along Bowen Island Trunk Road (Government Road), immediately coming to a junction with Cardena Drive. Note the 1924-built Tudor-style Bowen Island Public Library, which once served as a general store run by the Union Steamship Company. The company owned and operated 180 cottages, several picnic grounds, a dance pavilion, and an outdoor concert stage on the island. Much of its former lands became Crippen Regional Park in 1983.

South of the library near the marina entrance, you can follow the 0.2-km (0.1-mile) Lady Alexandra Promenade (named after one of the early luxury steamships servicing the Island) along Snug Cove and through the historical Davies Orchard (which once had platform tents and cottages for early vacationers) to the Dorman Point Trail. Then take

Big Sitka spruce along the Killarney Creek Trail

this steep-at-times, 1-km (0.6-mile) trail to a ridge above the cove and Dorman Point, with its views south to the mouth of Howe Sound and Vancouver's Point Grey Peninsula. This is a good spot for marine mammal sightings.

North of the library off Cardena Drive, you can hike the 0.3-km (0.2-mile) historical Causeway, enjoying excellent views of Deep Bay and a backdrop of peaks lining Howe Sound. Here, too, is the beginning of the Alder Grove Trail, providing access to the lovely Memorial Garden, as well as a few short spurs back to the Trunk Road and the paralleling Maple Trail.

The Alder Grove Trail traverses open forest along the lagoon, coming to a short spur leading to a fish ladder at tiny Bridal Veil Falls. At 0.8 km (0.5 mile), the trail reaches Miller Road. Head right here, crossing Killarney Creek, and pick up the Killarney Creek Trail, which travels through mature groves of cedars and Sitka spruces before reaching the outlet dam at Killarney Lake at 1.1 km (0.7 mile).

Several trails branch from Killarney Creek, including the 0.4-km (0.25-mile) Cedar Trail, which also leads to Killarney Lake. The 0.7-km (0.4-mile) Meadow Trail crosses the creek in grassy wetlands, providing views of Mount Gardner. The trail then passes the off-leash area and cuts across pretty Terminal Creek Meadows (former farmland that provided produce for vacationers) before coming to the Terminal Creek Hatchery. You can then return to the Alder Grove Trail via the 0.7-km (0.4-mile) Hatchery Trail, passing a massive and ancient cedar.

Hike or run around Killarney Lake on a wonderful 4-km (2.5-mile) loop trail (which uses a short stretch of dirt Magee Road). Enjoy excellent views of Mount Gardner across the lake and savor sections of serene shoreline. Along the lake's northern shoreline, the trail travels via boardwalks across attractive wetlands. Two trails diverge west from the loop trail, heading for Mount Gardner (Trail 16). Just west of the dam is a lovely picnic area, a perfect lunch spot for your day adventuring on the island.

A grand hike from the ferry terminal and back using the Alder Grove and Killarney Creek Trails, with a loop around Killarney Lake, comes in at 9 km (5.6 miles) roundtrip. If you return via the Meadow and Hatchery Trails, the loop total comes to 9.7 km (6 miles).

GO FARTHER

Strong hikers and runners can combine a hike at Crippen with an ascent of Mount Gardner.

16 Mount Gardner

DISTANCE:	15.7 km (9.8 miles) roundtrip
ELEVATION GAIN:	765 m (2510 feet)
HIGH POINT:	727 m (2385 feet)
DIFFICULTY:	Difficult
FITNESS:	Hikers
FAMILY-FRIENDLY:	Yes, older children
DOG-FRIENDLY:	On leash
AMENITIES:	Washrooms, picnic tables
CONTACT/MAPS:	Bowen Island Municipality
BEFORE YOU GO:	Mount Gardner is on Crown land, but its trails are maintained by the Bowen Island Trail Society, which has an excellent map on its website. Gardner's summit and higher elevations are subject to snow from December through March.
GPS:	N49.375 W123.271

GETTING THERE

Map to: Horseshoe Bay Ferry Terminal, West Vancouver, BC. **Transit:** TransLink buses 250, 257, 262 service Horseshoe Bay ferry terminal; 282 stops at Mount Gardner trailhead at Killarney Lake. **Parking:** Park in Horseshoe Bay ferry terminal lot 1621 (fee) and walk onto ferry for Snug Cove on Bowen Island.

A classic hike to the highest summit on Bowen Island, Mount Gardner grants sweeping, stunning views of Howe Sound, the Sunshine Coast, North Shore peaks, Mount Baker, the Vancouver skyline, and a whole lot more. En route to Gardner's two summits, explore ledges, remnant patches of old-growth trees, and seasonal creeks. And there's always a good chance of greeting a deer or two along the way.

GET MOVING

While you can shorten this hike by driving to the trailhead near the Killarney Lake picnic area, the greener and much

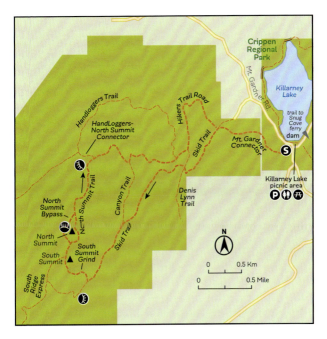

cheaper option is to start your hike from the Snug Cove ferry terminal. You still have the option of catching a bus to the trailhead from there, but service is infrequent. So, get an early start and plan for an all-day hike. From the ferry landing, walk to the Alder Grove Trail on Cardena Drive, just north of the library and visitor information center. Then hike Alder Grove to the Killarney Creek Trail and on to the Killarney Lake Loop (see Trail 15 for trail descriptions). Head left on the loop, passing the lake's dam, and arrive at the lake's picnic area at 2.6 km (1.6 miles). Then look for the opened-in-2022 (and not on most maps) Mount Gardner Connector trailhead on the west side of Mount Gardner Road. Take it!

Now start climbing gently through quiet woods. At 3.6 km (2.2 miles), come to a kiosk at the trailheads for Hiker's Trail Road and Skid (South Side) Trail at a paved road end. While the most direct approach up Gardner is via Hiker's Trail Road, I suggest a more varied loop. Continue left on the Skid Trail, hiking through second-growth cedars and hemlocks and crossing a few creeks. The way soon steepens, passing the Denis Lynn Trail and a connector to the Hiker's Trail Road.

Skirt talus and ledges as the grade eventually moderates, following an old logging (skid) road. Pass the Canyon Trail and jumbled boulders. At 6.6 km (4.1 miles), come to the South Summit Grind. Grunt up the Grind, steeply ascending on ledges and through rows of stately old trees. Pass a ledge adorned with shore pines that provides a window view east to Black Mountain, Burnaby Mountain, and Vancouver. At 7.4 km (4.6 miles), reach the viewless South Summit. Then make a short descent, coming to the South Ridge Express. Veer right, and at 7.7 km (4.8 miles), reach a junction with the North Summit Bypass. Head right on the North Summit Trail, and after a short, quick climb, reach the mountain's lower but view-granting summit at 8 km (5 miles).

Don't let the helipads or communications towers detract from the stunning views of the Sunshine Coast, Mount Elphinstone, Tetrahedron Peak, Keats Island, the Vancouver skyline, Point Grey, the San Juan and Gulf Islands, and Mount Baker. Soak up the scenery and then prepare to descend. Continuing north on the North Summit Trail, come to an insanely steep stretch aided by a rope. If it's too unnerving, retrace your steps from the North Summit and take the North Summit Bypass instead.

After making the rope-assist drop, reach another junction with the bypass at 8.3 km (5.2 miles). Then bear right, descending through old-growth forest and reaching a ledge with a spectacular view of the Sunshine Coast at 9.2 km (5.7 miles). Soon afterward, bear right at a junction where a connector trail drops steeply to the Handloggers Trail. A little beyond, the North Summit Trail reaches the Hiker's Trail Road. Follow this old service road on a decent grade, passing numerous trail junctions and returning to the kiosk junction at 12.1 km (7.5 miles). Then head down the Mount Gardner Connector, retracing your route back through Crippen Regional Park and arriving at the ferry terminal at 15.7 km (9.8 miles).

GO FARTHER

Consider taking the Handloggers Connector to the Handloggers Trail on the return for some solitude and a stretch of beautiful old-growth forest. This return adds another 1.5 km (0.9 mile) and 50 m (165 feet) of ascent to your total. Strong hikers and trail runners can expand their Gardner explorations on more trails.

Stunning view of Howe Sound and the North Shore Mountains

WEST VANCOUVER

17   Lighthouse Park

DISTANCE:	About 10 km (6.2 miles) of trails
ELEVATION GAIN:	Up to 260 m (850 feet)
HIGH POINT:	122 m (400 feet)
DIFFICULTY:	Easy to moderate
FITNESS:	Walkers, hikers
FAMILY-FRIENDLY:	Yes, but exercise caution on secondary trails and cliff-top viewpoints
DOG-FRIENDLY:	Yes, off leash if dog is well-behaved and stays on trails
AMENITIES:	Washrooms, interpretive signs, picnic tables, historical structures and lighthouse
CONTACT/MAPS:	District of West Vancouver Parks and Recreation
BEFORE YOU GO:	Open 7 AM to 10 PM
GPS:	N49.337 W123.263

GETTING THERE

Map to: Lighthouse Park Parking, West Vancouver, BC. **Transit:** TransLink bus 250 stops on Marine Drive at Beacon Lane. **Parking:** The parking lot on Beacon Lane often fills on sunny weekends, and you will be turned away. There is no parking along the access road.

Walk through one of the largest and most impressive tracts of primeval forest in Metropolitan Vancouver to coastal cliffs providing stunning views of strait, sound, summits, and city skyline. And admire the Point Atkinson Lighthouse, one of the most recognized and photographed landmarks in the Lower Mainland. With its rugged granite coastline, Lighthouse Park looks like it belongs in New Brunswick. But the towering mountains to its north shout Pacific Northwest.

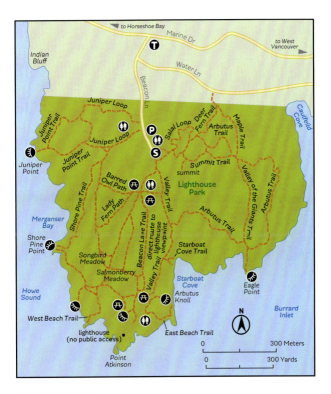

GET MOVING

Though a relatively small, 75-ha (185-acre) park, you can easily spend all day hiking and exploring here. If you're interested in just making a beeline to the lighthouse, follow the Beacon Lane Trail (service road) south for 0.8 km (0.5 mile) to the lighthouse complex. You can get a great close-up view and some good overlooking views of the 18-m (59-foot) lighthouse sitting on rocky Point Atkinson at the mouth of Burrard Inlet. A lighthouse first occupied this spot in 1874. This one has been in use since 1912 and is registered as a national historical site.

Also check out the historical structures at the point. There are six ancillary buildings, including one that served as a bunkhouse for the armed forces during World War II, when the lighthouse was used to surveil for enemy airplanes and watercraft.

As attractive as the lighthouse is, the real highlight here is the old-growth forest, one of the largest in Metro Vancouver. The park's arbutus trees are impressive too. The Valley of the Giants Trail is a must, with its monstrous Douglas-firs and western red cedars.

Lighthouse Park also contains numerous rocky bluffs and coastal cliffs granting stunning and sweeping views. From Eagle Point, look east across Burrard Inlet to the Vancouver skyline and Lions Gate Bridge, set against a snowy Mount Baker backdrop. Starboat Cove offers good views out to Point Grey Peninsula, while the West Beach ledges west of the lighthouse offer great views of the lighthouse and Vancouver Island, across the Strait of Georgia. Shore Pine Point and Juniper Point offer stunning views of the strait, little Passage Island, Bowen Island, and the mouth of Howe Sound. And bald eagles are common at all of these shoreline spots.

A nice loop in the park encompassing all the lookout spots via the Salal Loop, Arbutus Trail (or Valley of the Giants Trail), Valley Trail, West Beach Trail, Shore Pine Trail, Juniper Loop, and Juniper Point Trail is about 5.6 km (3.5 miles), with more than 305 m (1000 feet) of vertical climbing.

GO FARTHER

Drive 7.7 km (4.8 miles) northwest along Marine Drive to its terminus at Whytecliff Park and explore this small but lovely park at the mouth of Howe Sound. Walk its 2 km (1.2 miles) of trails. Scramble up coastal ledges. Watch BC Ferries and marine mammals ply the Queen Charlotte Channel, and when tides are low, hike out to tiny Whyte Islet.

Point Atkinson Lighthouse as seen from West Beach

18 Yew Lake and Black Mountain

DISTANCE:	2.3-km (1.4-mile) loop/9 km (5.6 miles) roundtrip
ELEVATION GAIN:	30 m (100 feet)/550 m (1800 feet)
HIGH POINT:	950 m (3117 feet)/1224 m (4016 feet)
DIFFICULTY:	Easy/difficult
FITNESS:	Walkers/hikers
FAMILY-FRIENDLY:	Yes, and Yew Lake is wheelchair-accessible
DOG-FRIENDLY:	Prohibited at Yew Lake; on leash at Black Mountain
AMENITIES:	Washrooms, water, interpretive signs, picnic tables, concessions during summer
CONTACT/MAPS:	Cypress Provincial Park; excellent free map available at park kiosks
BEFORE YOU GO:	Note gate closure times at Cypress Bowl ski area to avoid being locked in. Parking is also available before the gate. Trails are accessible and generally snow free from late June through October.
GPS:	N49.397 W123.205

GETTING THERE

Map to: Cypress Creek Lodge, West Vancouver, BC. **Parking:** Park in the large ski area parking lot.

Walk an easy loop through an alpine bog and spectacular groves of old-growth forest. Or toil up the infamous Baden-Powell Trail to Black Mountain, with its sublime subalpine lakes and Eagle Bluff. From Black's summit, enjoy a fine view of Howe Sound and the iconic Lions (Two Sisters). From the bluff, prepare to be blown away, staring more than 1000 m (3500 feet) straight down to the strait. Marvel at Howe Sound, Bowen Island, and the Vancouver skyline from one of the finest vantages in the Lower Mainland.

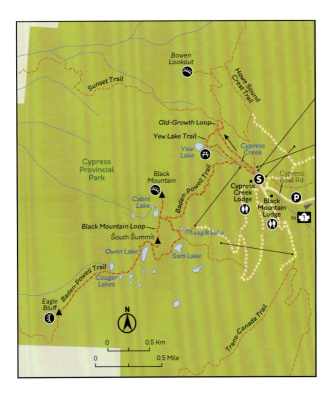

GET MOVING

Cypress Provincial Park, named for its Alaska yellow cedars (a member of the cypress family), provides some of the easiest access to old-growth forest in the Lower Mainland. Owing to the park's excellent trail system, proximity to Vancouver, and developed recreation (skiing in winter; mountain coaster in summer), expect lots of company. Yew Lake Trail is one of the park's more popular trails.

Yew Lake

Walk 0.2 km (0.1 mile) from the parking lot to just north of the Cypress Creek Lodge to kiosk 1 for the start of the

Jaw-dropping panorama from Eagle Bluff

barrier-free (wheelchair-accessible) Yew Lake Trail. Bear left at the Howe Sound Crest Trail (HSCT) junction, following Cypress Creek, and then right at a junction at 0.3 km (0.2 mile). Continue through groves of ancient mountain hemlocks, Alaska yellow cedars, and Douglas-firs. Note, too, the occasional western white pine. The trail soon traverses a large bog pocketed by wetland pools. In early season, admire a variety of flowering plants, including copious buck beans.

At 0.9 km (0.6 mile), come to a junction with the 0.4-km (0.3-mile) barrier-free Old-Growth Loop. You'll definitely want to take this loop, which winds through a fine grove of primeval forest. Then return to the Yew Lake Trail and at 1.6 km (1 mile), come to pretty Yew Lake and a couple of picnic sites at the base of Black Mountain. At 2.1 km (1.3 miles), cross Cypress Creek and come to the Baden-Powell Trail. Turn left to return to your start at 2.3 km (1.4 miles)—or turn right and start hiking to Black Mountain.

Black Mountain

Walk 0.2 km (0.1 mile) from the parking lot to just north of the Cypress Creek Lodge and pick up the Baden-Powell (B-P) Trail (see sidebar), following it west. The B-P Trail runs for 48 km (30 miles) across the North Shore Mountains, with some of its most challenging and scenic terrain here in Cypress Provincial Park.

Pass the Yew Lake Trail and then begin climbing, steeply at times, skirting the edge of ski slopes. The trail is rugged with lots of loose rock, but it gets much better. After passing a small pool, the climb eases. At 1.9 km (1.2 miles), reach a junction. You'll be returning on the B-P Trail to your left, so head right on the Black Mountain Loop, reaching Cabin Lake (enticing in summer) and a junction at 2.1 km (1.3 miles). Head right for 0.2 km (0.1 mile) to Black Mountain's northern and highest summit (elev. 1224 m/4016 feet) and enjoy a good view of The Lions (Two Sisters) and other Howe Sound peaks, as well as Howe Sound itself. But the best views lie farther ahead.

Return to the junction and keep hiking straight over the rocky, 1218-m (3996-foot) south summit. Then enter a thick hemlock forest and steeply descend, coming to a junction with the B-P Trail at 2.9 km (1.8 miles). You'll return on the lefthand trail, so for now head right, passing Owen Lake and enjoying fairly level and easy hiking across Black's high plateau. Traverse pocket meadows, primeval forest, and—with the help of boardwalks—bogs. After passing the small Cougar Lakes at 3.5 km (2.2 miles), begin descending, reaching the wide, open ledges of Eagle Bluff (elev. 1050 m/3445 feet) at 4.5 km (2.8 miles).

Now savor some of the finest views in the North Shore Mountains, particularly the one to the west, looking straight down to Horseshoe Bay, Howe Sound, and Bowen Island. Admire, too, the view out over the Strait of Georgia to Vancouver Island and the marvelous views south to Burrard Inlet with its flotilla of ocean liners, the Grey Peninsula behind it, and Mount Baker and the shimmering Vancouver skyline to the southeast. And after meeting the avian locals, you'll contemplate why the bluff is not named Raven instead of Eagle.

Now retrace your steps for 1.6 km (1 mile) to the Black Mountain Loop junction and keep right on the B-P Trail, coming to Sam and Theagill Lakes. Bear left at two junctions with trails leading to the ski slopes and start a short but steep climb, coming to the first Black Mountain Loop junction at 7.1 km (4.4 miles). Head right on a deep descent, returning to your start at 9 km (5.6 miles).

GO FARTHER

Strong hikers can follow the Howe Sound Crest Trail into some incredibly gorgeous, challenging, and out-of-the scope of-this-book terrain. Strong hikers can also follow the service road ski trail 3.7 km (2.3 miles) up to Mount Strachan's 1442-m (4731-foot) summit for sweeping views of nearly the entire Howe Sound Crest and so much more.

BADEN-POWELL TRAIL: SCOUTING A ROUTE ACROSS THE NORTH SHORE MOUNTAINS

The 48-km (30-mile) Baden-Powell Trail—referred to and marked along the way as the B-P Trail—starts in Horseshoe Bay in West Vancouver and finishes at Deep Cove in North Vancouver. It traverses some incredibly challenging terrain and several popular parks. While portions of the trail are well-graded with smooth tread, other sections are rocky, rooty, and steep.

The trail was constructed in 1971 to help commemorate the one-hundredth anniversary of British Columbia's entry into Canada as the country's sixth province. It was initiated by the Boy Scouts and Girl Guides of BC, with many of them doing the actual construction of the trail. The trail was named in honor of Robert Baden-Powell (Lord Baden-Powell), a British Army officer and writer who founded the worldwide Scout Movement in 1907. Well-traveled, Baden-Powell came to Canada on several occasions, including a stop in Vancouver during a cross-country tour in 1935.

Every summer, more than 250 runners participate in the annual Knee Knackering North Shore Trail Run, which follows the B-P trail from end to end, gaining and losing more than 2435 m (8000 feet) along the way. Runners have ten hours to complete the grueling course. The race is put on by the non-profit Northshore Ultra Trailrunning Society and to date has raised more than $132,000 for various charities.

This book features many parks that contain sections of the B-P Trail, including Cypress Provincial Park (Trails 18 and 19), Capilano River Regional Park (Trail 21), Grouse Mountain Regional Park (Trail 22), Lynn Canyon Park (Trail 23), Lynn Headwaters Regional Park (Trail 24), and the Lower Seymour Conservation Reserve (Trail 25).

19 Blue Gentian Lake and Hollyburn Mountain

DISTANCE:	5.2 km (3.2 miles)/10.2 km (6.3 miles) roundtrip
ELEVATION GAIN:	180 m (590 feet)/425 m (1395 feet)
HIGH POINT:	945 m (3100 feet) /1326 m (4350 feet)
DIFFICULTY:	Easy/moderate
FITNESS:	Hikers, runners
FAMILY-FRIENDLY:	Yes
DOG-FRIENDLY:	On leash
AMENITIES:	Washrooms, picnic tables, interpretive signs
CONTACT/MAPS:	Cypress Provincial Park; excellent free map available at park kiosks
BEFORE YOU GO:	Trails are generally accessible and snow free from late June through October.
GPS:	N49.379 W123.192

GETTING THERE

Map to: Cypress Mountain Hollyburn Nordic Area, West Vancouver, BC. **Parking:** The parking and trailhead are just before the Nordic center buildings on the Nordic Ski Access Road.

Follow a good network of well-graded trails through ski slopes, boggy meadows, and primeval forest to a couple of nice hikes through Cypress Provincial Park's popular Nordic skiing area. Hike to a series of small, placid lakes or to an inviting mountaintop granting an excellent view of the iconic Lions (Two Sisters) reigning over the Capilano River valley. Come in late summer and share the trail with the park's resident bears, drawn to the area's abundant berries.

GET MOVING

Winter recreationists have long been drawn to the mountains that now comprise Cypress Provincial Park. The park's alpine ski area, known as Cypress Mountain, consists of modern lodges and lifts servicing Black Mountain and Mount Strachan.

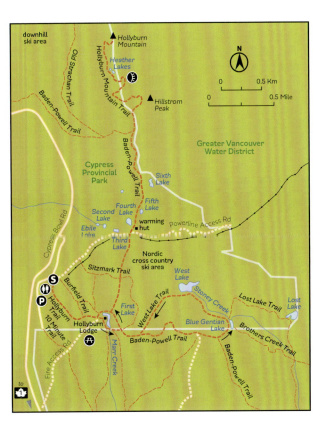

Cypress hosted the freestyle skiing and snowboarding competitions for the 2010 Winter Olympics. Cypress's Hollyburn Nordic ski area predates the park's alpine history by a half century. In summer, these old but still well-used ski runs make excellent hiking and running trails. And the trails on this section of the 3012-ha (7443-acre) park are much quieter than the ones near the downhill skiing center.

For a 5.2 mile loop to Blue Gentian Lake, follow the wide Hollyburn Trail (or the paralleling Burfield Trail for the same distance) from kiosk 3 on a gentle grade, coming to the historic Hollyburn Lodge on First Lake at 0.8 km (0.5 mile). This rustic but charming lodge was built in 1926, long before the park road opened in 1970. It was quite a trek to get here, warranting the need for accommodations. A ski jump once graced the hillside to the east of the lake.

Snoop around, then continue east around the south shore of First Lake, crossing Marr Creek on a bridge, and coming to the Baden-Powell (B-P) Trail at 1.1 km (0.7 mile). Proceed straight (east) on the B-P—here a double track—straddling the park boundary and passing numerous rustic ski cabins, many in existence long before the park's establishment in 1975. At 1.3 km (0.8 mile), come to the West Lake Trail, which you'll be returning on.

Stay on the B-P Trail, slowly descending and at times traversing boggy terrain. The way leaves the double track through a small opening and descends. Bend right at a junction where a short trail connects to the West Lake Trail. In old-growth forest at 2.3 km (1.4 miles), leave the B-P Trail, heading left and coming to pretty little Blue Gentian Lake (elev. 823 m/2700 feet) at 2.6 km (1.6 miles). Look for bog-loving gentians in late summer. Look, too, for sundews and laurels.

At the north end of the lake, three trails diverge. Take the one leading west to West Lake. Follow alongside Stoney Creek and climb in beautiful forest, passing the shortcut trail and reaching West Lake at 3.2 km (2 miles). The dammed lake is quite pretty, reflecting attractive conifers. When you're done admiring the lake, continue on the West Lake Trail on double track, returning to the B-P Trail at 3.9 km (2.4 miles). From here, retrace your steps 1.3 km (0.8 mile) to your start.

To ascend Hollyburn Mountain, follow the wide Hollyburn Trail (or the paralleling Burfield Trail for the same distance) from kiosk 3 to the historic Hollyburn Lodge on First Lake at 0.8 km (0.5 mile). Then follow a short trail along the lake's north shore, reaching the Baden-Powell (B-P) Trail at 1 km

Excellent view of The Lions (Two Sisters) from Hollyburn's summit

(0.6 mile). Turn left and follow it on double track through a wide ski swath graced with an abundance of huckleberry shrubs and berry-loving bears. Be bear aware here.

Pass the Sitzmark Trail and begin climbing, coming to a warming hut at the Powerline Access Road—a shorter approach to the mountain but far less interesting. Continue on the B-P Trail through the wide swath, gently climbing and passing little Fourth Lake and littler Fifth Lake. Sixth Lake lies hidden in the forest. The trail skirts the swath, at times traversing pretty groves of hemlock, fir, and Alaska yellow cedar.

At 3.1 km (1.9 miles), leave the B-P Trail for the Hollyburn Mountain Trail. Now climbing more steadily, soon leave the ski swath behind. The well-built trail wends through primeval forest, coming to a good viewpoint looking east at 4.3 km (2.7 miles). Look out at Burnaby Mountain, Indian Arm, the Port Mann Bridge, and Mount Baker. Then traverse a steep slope before reaching the tiny Heather Lakes, tucked in heather meadows beneath Hollyburn's summit block.

One last, steep grunt up some ledges remains before reaching Hollyburn's fairly broad summit at 5.1 km (3.2 miles). Trees block any wide-angle perspectives, but views are good out to Black Mountain, Mount Strachan, and Crown Mountain. The best view is from just north of the summit, past some ledges and a small tarn. Here, marvel at The Lions (Two Sisters) guarding the Capilano watershed, which makes up part of Metro Vancouver's water supply.

GO FARTHER

From Blue Gentian Lake, follow the Lost Lake Trail to Lost Lake and return via the Brothers Creek Trail for a 2.4-km (1.5-mile) loop. You can also access the Hollyburn Mountain Trail from the trailhead at the downhill ski area by following the B-P Trail east for 2 km (1.2 miles).

20 Centennial Seawalk and Ambleside Park

DISTANCE:	6.4 km (4 miles) roundtrip
ELEVATION GAIN:	Minimal
HIGH POINT:	6 m (20 feet)
DIFFICULTY:	Easy
FITNESS:	Walkers, runners, bicyclists
FAMILY-FRIENDLY:	Yes
DOG-FRIENDLY:	On leash and only on paved trails
AMENITIES:	Washrooms, picnic tables and shelters, playgrounds, tennis courts, sports fields, concessions, interpretive signs
CONTACT/MAPS:	District of West Vancouver Parks and Recreation
BEFORE YOU GO:	Parking limited along the seawall
GPS:	N49.322 W123.147

GETTING THERE

Map to: Ambleside Park, West Vancouver, BC. **Transit:** TransLink buses R2 (rapid line), 44, 250, 251, 252, 253, 254, 255, 256, 257. **Parking:** Parking limited along the seawall; park at Ambleside Park or use street parking (paid and free available).

Walk along Metro Vancouver's "other seawall," enjoying sweeping views across Burrard Inlet to "the Seawall." Take in stunning views of Stanley Park and the Lions Gate Bridge, as well as the Point Grey Peninsula and North Shore Mountains. Stop along the way to check out beaches, piers, historical points and structures, birds, and marine mammals. This hike is never far from the Ambleside neighborhood's restaurants and galleries, so plan on a diversion or two.

GET MOVING

From the end of Argyle Avenue, locate the seawall trail at Ambleside Park's popular Dog Beach. Here at the confluence

of the Capilano River and Burrard Inlet, sandbars and spits form, creating good beach terrain. To the left, the trail continues north as the Capilano Pacific Trail, traveling along the Capilano River (see Trail 21). You want to head right (west) on a paved path paralleling Argyle Avenue and a string of beaches.

Enjoy excellent close-up views of the Lions Gate Bridge. Opened in 1938 and financed by the Guinness family (yes, the same one that produced the notorious ale), the bridge helped stimulate development in West Vancouver—especially for the British Pacific Properties corporation (which Guinness was an investor in). The company acquired 4000 acres during the Great Depression and continues to add neighborhoods to the city today.

Continue along sandy beach, passing the 4.9-m (16-foot) Squamish Nation *Welcome Figure*, carved in old-growth timber by Squamish master carver and elder, Sequiliem (Stan Joseph). If it's summer, the beach will be packed—and the trail is always busy on a sunny evening. At 0.6 km (0.4 mile), come to the Hollyburn Sailing Club and a junction with the Spirit Trail. The paved Spirit Trail, heading east, offers a bicycle bypass through Ambleside Park; for a shorter hike, you can use it to loop back 1.5 km (0.9 mile) to your start.

Otherwise, continue west on the Spirit Trail (shared with Argyle Avenue), passing (or checking out) the Ambleside Pier and reaching Millennium Park at 0.9 km (0.6 mile). Bear left off the Spirit Trail and return to the shore, passing the Silk Purse Arts Centre. Little Millennium Park can be busy with music and art events, and it's the only park in West Vancouver where alcohol can be consumed legally (but responsibly).

The trail soon enters the popular John Lawson Park, named after one of West Vancouver's original pioneers. The park is home to playgrounds, a small pier, and the Navvy Jack House, which was built in 1872 and is the city's oldest homestead. The first non-Indigenous resident of West Vancouver, Navvy Jack ran a ferry system and mined and supplied the region with washed pea gravel, which in British Columbia is referred to by his name.

Walkers amble through John Lawson Park.

Pass the Seawalk Garden and begin paralleling a railroad line and seaside residences. You are now officially on the Centennial Seawalk. Enjoy sweeping views from Point Atkinson to the Vancouver skyline. Let your dog loose (but kept under control) on a parallel, gated, off-leash trail. After rounding Navvy Jack Point, the trail bends northwest, revealing views of Black Mountain and the tiered neighborhood below it. Pass a few neighborhood access points before coming to the seawalk's end at 3.2 km (2 miles) at Dundarave Park. Check out the pier and beach here before retracing your steps.

GO FARTHER

From the Ambleside Dog Beach, follow the Capilano Pacific Trail north for 6.5 km (4 miles) to the Cleveland Dam in Capilano River Regional Park (Trail 21).

NORTH VANCOUVER

21 Capilano River Regional Park

DISTANCE:	About 17 km (10.5 miles) of trails
ELEVATION GAIN:	Up to 305 m (1000 feet)
HIGH POINT:	205 m (675 feet)
DIFFICULTY:	Easy to moderate
FITNESS:	Walkers, runners, hikers
FAMILY-FRIENDLY:	Yes, but keep kids close near river canyon
DOG-FRIENDLY:	Both on-leash and off-leash (but under control) trails. Note trail signs for regulations.
AMENITIES:	Washrooms, picnic tables and shelters, hatchery, interpretive signs
CONTACT/MAPS:	Metro Vancouver Regional Parks
BEFORE YOU GO:	Open 7 AM to dusk
GPS:	N49.356 W123.110

GETTING THERE

Map to: Capilano River Hatchery, North Vancouver, BC. **Transit:** TransLink buses 232, 236, 247. **Parking:** Park at the trailhead near the fish hatchery. Additional parking along Capilano Park Road and at Cleveland Dam trailhead.

Walk along the rim and into the depths of a deep, narrow canyon booming with the sounds of the roiling waters of the Capilano River. Hike across a towering dam, enjoying one of the finest views of the Lower Mainland's iconic Lions (Two Sisters). Admire pools, rapids, and steep granite falls. And wander among magnificent, primeval giants that were spared from the axes of early loggers.

GET MOVING

Not to be confused with the popular and historic Capilano Suspension Bridge Park (see sidebar), the adjacent Capilano River Regional Park is oft overlooked by the bridge park's million-plus annual visitors. The regional park, however, encompasses most of Capilano River's famous canyon, with its walls exceeding 40 m (130 feet). And within this 162-ha (400-acre) park, an extensive trail network allows you to explore the canyon.

From the hatchery (which is open to the public), choose from several trails to begin your explorations. The popular 1.1-km (0.7-mile) Coho Loop involves crossing the river on the high Cable Pool and Pipeline Bridges and offers excellent close-up views of canyon ledges, the cable pool, and river rapids. Named after the supreme chief of the Squamish People, whose headquarters were at the mouth of the river on Burrard Inlet, the Capilano River is popular with whitewater kayakers.

A right turn at the Cable Pool Bridge follows the 0.3-km (0.2-mile) Second Canyon Trail, providing impressive, close-up views of Cleveland Dam (91 m/299 feet tall) and the narrow, towering canyon walls below it. From Second Canyon, follow the 0.3-km (0.2-mile) Giant Fir Trail on a steep set of steps to impressive, towering old-growth cedars and Douglas-firs—including Grandfather Capilano (61 m/200 feet tall)—which escaped the rampant logging here in the early twentieth century.

From Giant Fir, hike the Pipeline Trail for 1 km (0.6 mile) south, crossing the canyon on the Pipeline Bridge and then following the water pipeline through mature second growth almost all the way to the park's southern entrance. Return on

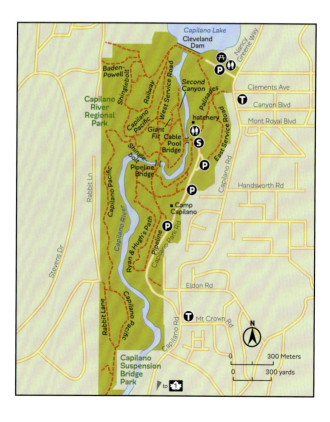

The Second Canyon Trail provides a look up the narrow chasm to Cleveland Dam.

the challenging, scenic 1-km (0.6-mile) Ryan & Hugh's Path over steep steps, rocks, and roots through tall timber along the precipitous canyon rim.

On the north side of the Pipeline Bridge, the 0.9-km (0.5-mile) Shinglebolt Trail travels along the canyon rim, granting excellent views down to the river. This trail connects to the Capilano Pacific Trail (more on this below) before climbing steeply to connect with the 0.5-km (0.3-mile) Railway Trail (which follows an old logging rail line) and the Baden-Powell Trail (see sidebar).

Be sure to walk over the 1954-built Cleveland Dam (site of several TV and film shoots) for excellent views down the spillway and across Capilano Lake (one of Metro Vancouver's main water supplies) to the majestic Lions (Two Sisters) rising above. You can return to the hatchery by following the gentle East Service Road and steep Palisades Trail for 0.8 km (0.5 mile).

CAPILANO SUSPENSION BRIDGE PARK: VANCOUVER'S ORIGINAL ADVENTURE PARK

One of Metro Vancouver's most popular sights and parks is a privately owned bridge. But the Capilano Suspension Bridge Park isn't any old bridge and park (well, it actually is pretty old), but a truly unique part of the Vancouver experience. You'd be hard-pressed to find a district resident who has not been to this attraction.

In 1888, Scottish civil engineer and land developer George Grant Mackay purchased 2428 ha (6000 acres) of land encompassing the Capilano River canyon. A year later, Mackay—with the help of Squamish Chief August Jack Khahtsahlano (whom the Kitsilano Beach and Vancouver neighborhood are named for)—constructed a footbridge made of hemp rope and cedar planks, suspending it 137 m (450 feet) across the canyon and 70 m (230 feet) above the river. It soon became a popular destination for adventurous tourists.

The original bridge was replaced by a wire cable bridge in 1903. And the property has changed hands several times over the years, with each new owner reinforcing the bridge and making additions to the property, including a tea house and local First Nations totem poles. In 1956, the bridge was completely rebuilt (this is the version currently in place) and soon became a huge tourist attraction.

Current owner Nancy Stibbard purchased the property in 1983 and has transformed it into a world-class destination that attracts more than 1.2 million visitors a year. Along with the historic bridge in the 11-ha (27-acre) park, you can check out a couple of restaurants, a gift shop, the totem pole collection, and exhibits. Other park attractions include the Treetops Adventure canopy walk, which hovers a hundred feet above the forest floor; the Living Forest boardwalk, which winds through towering mature conifers; and the vertigo-inducing Cliffwalk, suspended directly over the canyon floor via cantilevers built right into the canyon wall. During the holiday season, the entire park is set aglow with lights. And while the park is not a hiking destination, it's easy to walk a few kilometers during your visit.

The Capilano Pacific Trail runs the entire length of the river, from the dam to Burrard Inlet. From the dam, follow a well-graded service road, intersect the Shinglebolt Trail, and then traverse steep canyon walls, making bridged crossings over cascading tributaries. At 2.3 km (1.4 miles), intersect the Rabbit Lane Trail (leading to a neighborhood) and skirt the fenced Capilano Suspension Bridge Park. Then traverse some private holdings and duck under Trans-Canada Highway 1 at 3.5 km (2.2 miles). The route then follows Keith Road for 0.5 km (0.3 mile) and returns to trail, reaching and traveling along a now much wider river. From here, travel past some historical buildings, dart under Marine Drive and Taylor Way, and skirt the 1950-built Park Royal Shopping Centre (the oldest mall in Canada) before reaching Ambleside Park (see Trail 20) and terminating at 6.4 km (4 miles) at the seawall trail.

22 Grouse Grind

DISTANCE:	2.5 km (1.6 miles) one-way
ELEVATION GAIN:	800 m (2625 feet)
HIGH POINT:	1090 m (3575 feet)
DIFFICULTY:	Challenging
FITNESS:	Runners, hikers
FAMILY-FRIENDLY:	No
DOG-FRIENDLY:	Prohibited on Grouse Grind and BCMC Route; allowed on leash on the Baden-Powell Trail
AMENITIES:	None; washrooms available at adjacent Grouse Mountain Skyride tram station
CONTACT/MAPS:	Metro Vancouver Regional Parks
BEFORE YOU GO:	Trail generally open May through October (check hours) and subject to closure during inclement weather. Grouse Grind is one-way up only. Return via BCMC Route or take the Grouse Mountain Skyride down (fee). Purchase tickets online or at the Alpine Guest Services in the Peak Chalet at adjacent Grouse Mountain Resort.
GPS:	N49.371 W123.098

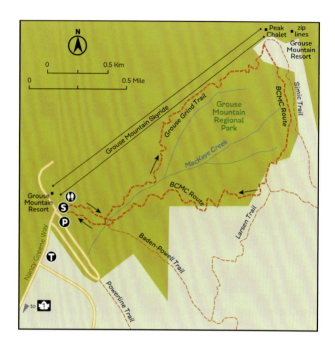

GETTING THERE

Map to: Grouse Mountain Skyride, North Vancouver, BC.
Transit: TransLink buses 232, 236, 247. **Parking:** You'll find pay
parking lots at the base of Grouse Mountain and can use the
PayByPhone app on your phone. Limited free street parking.

Touted as Mother Nature's Stairmaster, the Grouse Grind is
a grueling grunt involving 2830 steps up the steep western
face of Grouse Mountain. It's extremely popular, attracting
diehard locals and folks from afar (more than 100,000 annu-
ally) of all backgrounds to challenge their stamina. Summit
views are rewarding and there is a lot to check out at trail's
end, including a grizzly bear enclosure. Then take the Skyride
tram back to your start or hike some more and return on the
not quite as steep BCMC Route.

GET MOVING

Be greeted by numerous signs warning of risks, proper prepa-
rations, and trail rules—no dogs and no audible music among
them. Originally built in the 1980s by a couple of local climbers as a rough winter conditioning route, the grind has since
been reconstructed (with major upgrades in 2023-2024) and
is now part of the MVRD park system. Pass a scanner (which
reads Grind Timer Cards purchased from the ski area to record
your name and time). Most folks take around two hours; the
fastest known time is 23:48 for men and 29:10 for women.
Immediately veer left at a junction where the Baden-Powell
(B-P) trail heads right. Then start grinding through a mature
second-growth conifer forest. At 0.3 km (0.2 mile), come to a
junction. The BCMC Route heads straight. Head left under an
arch and let the fun begin as you ascend steeply at a grade
averaging 30 percent. The well-built wooden and stone steps
are relentless. Trail markers give distance in fortieths (i.e. GG
5/40) and larger signs state elevation progress in quarters.
At the one-quarter mark, assess your condition and turn
around if desired. Otherwise, continue on a much narrower,
steeper, and uphill-only route.

Ski netting along steeper stretches prevents a slip turning
into a tumble, and ropes holding the netting in place make for
nice hoisting assists. Window views through the trees reveal
Capilano Lake straight below. At 2.5 km (1.6 miles), reach the
Grind's terminus at the Peak Chalet (ski lodge). Relish in your
accomplishment, snap your selfies, and enjoy the excellent
view west over West Vancouver, Burrard Inlet, and Point Grey.

Now either catch the Skyride back down the mountain or
stay awhile. Grab lunch or coffee at the lodge. Check out the
two resident grizzly bears. Watch a bird or lumberjack show.
Ride a zip line (fee). Hike 1.5 km (0.9 mile) to the Eye of the
Wind Turbine (fee to enter) at the top of 1250 m (4100 ft)
Grouse Mountain and enjoy widespread views of adjacent
North Shore Mountains, the entire Greater Vancouver Metro

Nature's Stairmaster!

area, Vancouver Island, the Gulf Islands; and Washington's San Juan Islands, Mount Baker, and the North Cascades.

If intent on hiking back (trekking poles advised), follow the 2.9 km (1.8 miles) BCMC Route down the mountain. You will return to the Grind near a big gully 0.3 km (0.2 mile) from the trailhead. It's a slightly less steep trail than the Grouse Grind, mainly on good steps with a few rough and rocky stretches.

Want more? Follow the dog-friendly (on leash) Baden-Powell Trail east to a network of North Vancouver District Trails. Return to the trailhead on the Powerline Trail for a loop.

23 Lynn Canyon Park

DISTANCE:	More than 11 km (7 miles) of trails
ELEVATION GAIN:	Up to 250 m (820 feet)
HIGH POINT:	205 m (675 feet)
DIFFICULTY:	Easy to moderate
FITNESS:	Walkers, runners, hikers
FAMILY-FRIENDLY:	Yes, but keep kids close near river canyon
DOG-FRIENDLY:	Both on-leash and off-leash (but under control) trails. Note trail signs for regulations.
AMENITIES:	Washrooms, picnic tables, interpretive signs, ecology center, café
CONTACT/MAPS:	Lynn Canyon Ecology Centre, District of North Vancouver Parks, Trails, & Recreation
BEFORE YOU GO:	Open 7 AM to 6 PM in winter; 6 AM to 10 PM in summer.
GPS:	N49.343 W123.019

GETTING THERE

Map to: Lynn Canyon Ecology Centre, North Vancouver, BC.
Transit: TransLink buses 227, 228. **Parking:** Fee to park March 1 to October 31, four hours maximum. Parking fills fast on summer days. Consider alternative parking areas on Lillooet Road (see Trail 25), with no fees or maximum hours.

Famous for its historic, thrilling, and perhaps unnerving suspension bridge, Lynn Canyon is one of the oldest and most popular parks in Metropolitan Vancouver. Most visitors congregate at the bridge or take a short hike to the Twin Falls or 30 Foot Pool. But there are kilometers of trails beyond. Amble along the crashing Lynn Creek and through misty, luxuriant, second-growth temperate rainforest to escape the crowds.

GET MOVING

Before hitting the trails, check out the Ecology Centre (donation requested) to learn more about the region. Opened in

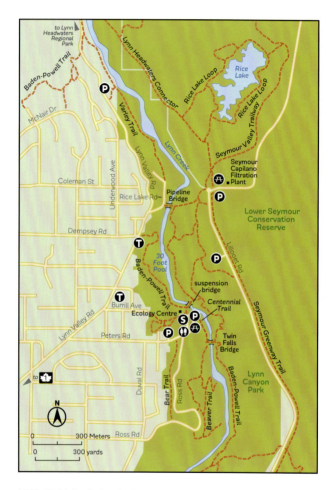

1971 (British Columbia's centennial), the center is shaped like a Pacific dogwood blossom, the provincial flower. Lynn Canyon Park itself opened much earlier, in 1912. After the area was extensively logged by the McTavish brothers, they donated a small parcel of land to the district for a park and built a suspension bridge, in hopes of attracting prospective buyers to their real estate development. The bridge became a big draw and required a twelve-cent fee (about the equivalent of four dollars today) to cross.

Much has changed since then. The park's original infrastructure was destroyed in 1919 when large chunks of land slid into the canyon during weeks of torrential rains. The park, however, has grown from 5 ha (12 acres) to 250 ha (617 acres). The bridge is still in place (since reinforced), and it's now free to cross.

Head to the bridge and enjoy being suspended across tight Lynn Canyon 50 m (164 feet) above the tumbling creek below. Be astounded—or possibly unnerved when it's packed with people and really starts to bounce and sag. Take your obligatory selfies and then explore the trails. Note the many signs warning not to jump into the canyon. Lynn Canyon is well known to local paramedics. Scores of folks have died or been badly injured here due to unsafe behavior. Don't be one of them.

Check out the short, 1.1-km (0.7-mile) Twin Falls Loop, which includes two bridges over the canyon (the suspension bridge being one), segments of the Baden-Powell (B-P) and Centennial Trails, and lots of steps and beautiful boardwalks. Enjoy a remnant grove of old-growth forest and close-up views of Twin Falls, which impede salmon from swimming farther upriver. The Pipeline Bridge Loop also involves two canyon crossings (the suspension bridge being one), a good number of steps, and a long stretch of boardwalk. This 2.1-km (1.3-mile) loop takes you past the green-sheened 30 Foot Pool and safe wading spots. It involves a short road walk and a stint on the B-P Trail. Alternatively, skip the road walk and loop back to the suspension bridge via a pleasant forest trail to the east.

For quiet ramblings, check out the self-guided Bear Trail (pick up the brochure for a fee in the Ecology Centre) and adjacent wood roads in the park's southwest.

GO FARTHER

For longer quiet ramblings, follow the B-P Trail south from the suspension bridge for 1.4 km (0.9 mile). Then continue on the Sea to Sky Trail, following Lynn Creek for 5.6 km (3.5 miles) through Inter River Park and Bridgman Park to the trail's terminus in Harbourview Park, at the river's industrial confluence with Burrard Inlet.

Alternatively, you can hike and run a long way by continuing to adjacent Lynn Headwaters Regional Park (Trail 24) and Lower Seymour Conservation Reserve (Trail 25) and their excellent networks of trails. The adjacent CMHC Mountain Forest appeals more to mountain bikers.

Stairway built along the canyon wall along the Baden-Powell Trail

24 Lynn Headwaters Regional Park

DISTANCE:	More than 40 km (25 miles) of trails
ELEVATION GAIN:	Up to 800 m (2630 feet)
HIGH POINT:	993 m (3260 feet)
DIFFICULTY:	Easy to strenuous
FITNESS:	Walkers, runners, hikers
FAMILY-FRIENDLY:	Yes
DOG-FRIENDLY:	Both on-leash and off-leash (but under control) trails. Note trail signs for regulations.
AMENITIES:	Washrooms, picnic tables, interpretive signs, historical sites
CONTACT/MAPS:	Metro Vancouver Regional Parks
BEFORE YOU GO:	Open 7 AM to dusk
GPS:	N49.360 W123.028

GETTING THERE

Map to: Lynn Headwaters Entrance Parking, North Vancouver, BC. **Transit:** TransLink bus 228 stops at corner of Dempsey Road and Lynn Valley Road, requiring a 1.6-km (1-mile) walk via Rice Lake Road and Varley Trail to park entrance. **Parking:** Fee to park March 1 to October 31. Parking fills fast on summer days and weekends. Free overflow parking areas (Cedar Mills Trail Parking) along Lynn Valley Road before park entrance.

The largest park in Metro Vancouver Regional District, Lynn Headwaters contains more than 3700 ha (9200 acres) of rugged and wild terrain cradling the upper Lynn Creek watershed. Hike along the crashing creek, catching gorgeous views of the steep, craggy flanks of peaks lining the tight river valley. Most of the big conifers were logged more than a century ago—but you can still admire big cottonwoods, big boulders, and a big, beautiful waterfall.

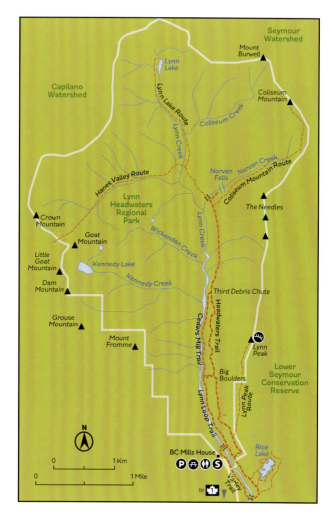

GET MOVING

Lynn Headwaters Regional Park sits at an abrupt transition between urban and wild. Much of this park is rugged wilderness traversed by a handful of extremely challenging routes, appropriate only for experienced hikers, scramblers, and climbers. Those destinations—including Coliseum Mountain, Lynn Lake, and the Hanes Valley Route—are out of the scope of this book. But there's plenty of other terrain in Lynn Headwaters for this book to cover.

From the park entrance, follow a wide path, immediately coming to the historic BC Mills House. Built in 1908, it was the first prefabricated house on the North Shore and served as a residence, a schoolhouse, and the political headquarters of the satirical (but legitimate) Rhino Party. The home was eventually restored and moved to the park to serve as a museum (hours vary).

The path next crosses roiling Lynn Creek below the ruins of a water intake dam and immediately reaches a junction with the easy and popular Lynn Loop Trail. Follow this 5.6 km (3.5 mile) route left along the gorgeous creek before making a short, steep climb and returning to the trailhead through mature forest on slopes high above the river. A short spur leads to the Big Boulders.

A longer, even prettier loop can be made by ignoring the short climb and continuing along the creek, now on the Cedars Mill Trail. On boardwalks, steps, and good tread, you'll pass big cedar stumps, testimony to a mill that operated here in the 1920s. You'll also pass mature hemlocks and clearings along the creek that provide beautiful views of the formidable peaks hemming the waterway. The trail ends at a junction with the Headwaters Trail in rocky Third Debris Chute. For the loop, turn right and follow rougher tread on an up-and-down route, traversing ravines and a forested bench. Then continue on the Lynn Loop's upper level to complete a 9.4-km (5.8-mile) loop.

Strong hikers will want to continue left from Third Debris Chute on the Headwaters Trail, traveling deeper up the Lynn Creek valley. Pulling away from the creek, gently ascend, traversing second-growth rainforest and the impressive stumps of the grand forest that was once here. Pass the ruins of an old cabin and cross several deep gullies via bridges. At 2.9 km (1.8 miles) from the Third Debris Chute junction, just beyond the Coliseum Mountain Route (strictly for experienced scramblers), reach a suspension bridge over Norvan Creek. Follow a trail here leading right along Norvan Creek for 0.2 km (0.1 mile) to beautiful Norvan Falls. You can hike to the 30-m (98-foot) falls year-round, but it's exceptionally beautiful during the wetter months. Return along the upper loop trails for a grand, 15.6-km (9.7-mile) hike.

For a delightful and easy loop starting from the park entrance, head out on the Varley Trail (named for former area resident Frederick Varley, a member of the Canadian landscape painter collective known as the Group of Seven). Following it south along Lynn Creek, come to the Pipeline

Cedar Mills Trail along Lynn Creek

Bridge (see Trail 23) at 1.5 km (0.9 mile). Cross the bridge, entering the Lower Seymour Conservation Reserve (Trail 25). At 2 km (1.2 miles), head north on an old woods road, returning to the Lynn Loop Trail at 2.9 km (1.8 miles). From here, it's 0.5 km (0.3 mile) back to the trailhead.

GO FARTHER

Fit and experienced hikers can tackle the Lynn Peak Route (usually snow free from May through October). From the trailhead, it's a 4.6-km (2.9-mile) grunt, climbing 800 m (2625 feet) to the 992-meter (3255-foot) summit with its views of the Seymour River valley below and Mount Seymour (see Trail 26) across the valley.

25 Lower Seymour Conservation Reserve

DISTANCE:	More than 65 km (40 miles) of trails
ELEVATION GAIN:	Up to 550 m (1800 feet)
HIGH POINT:	280 m (920 feet)
DIFFICULTY:	Easy to moderate
FITNESS:	Walkers, runners, hikers, bicyclists
FAMILY-FRIENDLY:	Yes, and several trails wheelchair- and jogging stroller–accessible
DOG-FRIENDLY:	Yes, off leash (but under control) if south of Homestead Trail. Dogs prohibited north of Homestead and Lynn Headwaters Connector Trails.
AMENITIES:	Washrooms, water, picnic tables, interpretive signs, historical sites, fish hatchery
CONTACT/MAPS:	Metro Vancouver Regional Parks
BEFORE YOU GO:	Open 6 AM to various hours, ranging from 5 PM in winter to 9 PM in summer. All vehicles must be out of the lower gate on Lillooet Road by the posted closing time. Good equestrian trails.
GPS:	N49.351 W123.016

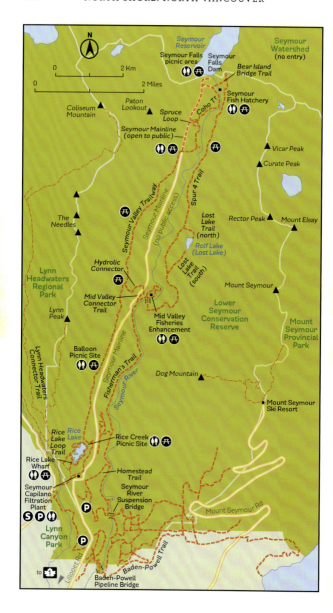

GETTING THERE

Map to: Seymour-Capilano Filtration Plant, North Vancouver, BC. **Parking:** Park at the filtration plant. Alternative parking lots can be found along Lillooet Road.

A massive preserve protecting one of Metro Vancouver's main water supplies, the Lower Seymour Conservation Reserve (LSCR) is also a recreational hot spot. Cyclists love its long trails to the Seymour Falls Dam, while walkers and hikers flock to Rice Lake and the kilometers of lovely trails along the salmon-spawning Seymour River. Strong hikers and runners can make it to the reserve's exceptional stand of old-growth forest.

GET MOVING

The LSCR stretches between two lofty rows of craggy peaks protecting 5668 ha (14,006 acres) of the Seymour River valley below Seymour Falls Dam. Bordering Lynn Headwaters Regional Park, Lynn Canyon Park, and Mount Seymour Provincial Park, the LSCR helps form a sprawling ecological and recreational swath across the District of North Vancouver. Extensively logged in the early twentieth century, this former demonstration forest is now managed by the Metro Water Services department due to its water reserve and its educational, recreational, and environmental values.

There are more than 65 km (40 miles) of trails in the LSCR, but most casual walkers and hikers will find it difficult to reach parts of the reserve without the aid of a bicycle. The paved Seymour Valley Trailway (SVT) extends 10 km (6.2 miles) from the main trailhead to the Seymour Mainline, from where it's another paved 1.8 km (1.1 miles) to the Seymour Falls Dam and Seymour Fish Hatchery. The SVT also offers access to the 2.3-km (1.4-mile) Coho Trail, which traverses the reserve's exceptional stand of primeval forest (including towering Sitka spruces) along the shores and channels of the river. The SVT is popular with cyclists, but strong hikers and runners will also enjoy this rolling path. Wheelchair-accessible washrooms and picnic tables are intermittently located along the way. The picnic area overlooking the Seymour Falls Dam also has drinking water.

Just below the dam creating the Seymour Reservoir (which provides water for several cities in the regional district), find the Bear Island Bridge. From the bridge, you can access the Spur 4 Trailway. This old dirt service road travels along the east side of the river, offering a different return. Two spurs lead off it to access Rolf Lake (Lost Lake), whose shoreline is choked with vegetation and downed logs. The

Placid Rice Lake

Spur 4 Trailway crosses the Seymour River 8.2 km (5.1 miles) from the Bear Island Bridge, reaching the Mid Valley Fisheries Enhancement. Here you can hike a 1.1-km (0.7-mile) loop around a wildlife-rich floodplain along the river and marshes. Views are good of the surrounding peaks. Also here, a short connector trail leads back to the SVT, while the Fisherman's Trail heads south, traveling along the river.

At 4.8 km (3 miles) from the Mid Valley Fisheries Enhancement, the Fisherman's Trail connects to the 1-km (0.6-mile) Homestead Trail, which leads back to the main trailhead. The Homestead Trail, along with the Fisherman's Trail south of this junction and the Twin Bridges Trail, is used to form a popular 3.7-km (2.3-mile) loop. Fisherman's Trail continues, passing an old homestead and pipeline tunnel and providing access to the Seymour River Suspension Bridge, built in 2018 at the site of the old Twin Bridges.

From the suspension bridge, the Fisherman's Trail continues south on the river's east bank, connecting to a series of popular mountain biking trails and the Baden-Powell (B-P) Trail at 1.6 km (1 mile) from the bridge. The B-P Trail crosses the river on the Baden-Powell Pipeline Bridge and at 1 km (0.6 mile), connects to the Berm Trail, which you can follow 1.8 km (1.1 miles) back to the main trailhead.

The most popular hike at LSCR is the 3.2-km (2-mile) Rice Lake Loop. You can access the loop either via the SVT or from the Lynn Headwaters Connector Trail. Rice Lake is an old reservoir that has been rehabilitated to a more natural state. The trail is wheelchair-accessible and has a wharf and two picnic areas along it.

GO FARTHER

Combine a hike around Rice Lake with the Lynn Loop Trail (see Trail 24) or a trip to the Lynn Canyon Suspension Bridge (see Trail 23). LSCR's popular Dog Mountain Trail is accessible from Mount Seymour (see Trail 26).

26 Mount Seymour

DISTANCE:	8.4 km (5.2 miles) roundtrip
ELEVATION GAIN:	540 m (1770 feet)
HIGH POINT:	1449 m (4754 feet)
DIFFICULTY:	Moderate
FITNESS:	Runners, hikers
FAMILY-FRIENDLY:	Yes, but use caution with young children
DOG-FRIENDLY:	On leash
AMENITIES:	Washrooms, picnic tables, ski lifts
CONTACT/MAPS:	BC Provincial Parks
BEFORE YOU GO:	The Loop to Mount Seymour is snow free from July through October. Other park trails outside of ski area are open in winter for snowshoeing and cross-country skiing but require a free day-use vehicle pass (to control crowding); check park website for dates and details. Always check avalanche warnings and park notices and closures.
GPS:	N49.368 W122.949

GETTING THERE

Map to: Mount Seymour Resort, North Vancouver, BC. **Parking:** Park in the last parking lot at the ski area. Alternative parking in lower lots.

This is one of the most popular hikes in the Lower Mainland, and for good reason. Start from a high base, travel a short way, and soak up stunning scenery in every direction. Views stretch from Mount Baker to Mount Garibaldi and across to the San Juan and Gulf Islands, with the entire Metro Vancouver area spread out directly below on Burrard Inlet and the Fraser River delta. You truly do see more on Seymour. Though short, the hike is rocky with lots of ups and downs.

GET MOVING

One of the more prominent and recognizable peaks rising above Metropolitan Vancouver, Mount Seymour's three

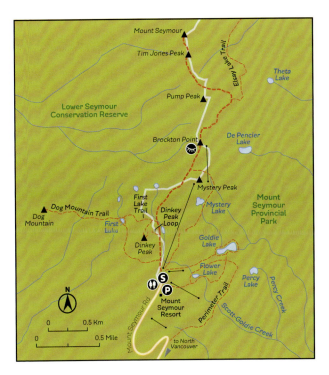

summits grant some of the best sweeping, jaw-dropping views of Canada's West Coast metropolis. The centerpiece of the 3509-ha (8671-acre) Mount Seymour Provincial Park, the peak was named for Frederick Seymour, who served as the second governor of the colony of British Columbia—a tenure that included overseeing unification with the colony of Vancouver Island.

The park was established in 1936. Two years later, skiing operations began on the mountain. But just beyond the ski lifts and communications towers is a rugged wilderness. And due to this mountain's accessibility, North Shore Rescue (NSR) teams have been kept plenty busy. Other than Mount Seymour, and the trails near the ski area and access road, the

Reflection pools on Mount Seymour's summit

rest of the park is out of the scope of this book. Take the Ten Essentials with you and heed weather and other park warnings while hiking here.

The trail to Mount Seymour begins at an elevation of 1020 m (3350 feet) at the north end of parking lot 4. Head north on the wide trail, skirting a ski run and the Mystery Peak Express chairlift. Pass a memorial to Tim Jones, a well-respected NSR leader who died of cardiac arrest here in 2014. Jones was responsible for saving hundreds of lives in the North Shore Mountains.

Ignore trails leading left to Dog Mountain, Dinkey Peak, and First Lake (see Go Farther below) and continue steadily climbing. After briefly following along a ski run, the way bends left on single track descending to a small pond. It then steadily climbs, reaching Brockton Point and its stunning views of Mount Baker above the Fraser River valley.

After crossing a couple of small creeks, the way bends left at a junction with the Elsay Lake Trail (strictly for experienced hikers) and gets steeper and rockier. At 3.2 km (2 miles), emerge on open ridge just below the summit block of 1407-m (4615-foot) Pump Peak (First Summit), named by an early climber for a summit tree resembling a water pump. It's a short scramble best approached from the west. The trail continues north, slightly descending before climbing onto a shoulder of Tim Jones Peak (Second Summit). A short spur leads right to the summit, with its excellent views of Mount Seymour before you. This is a good spot to turn around if young children are hiking with you.

The Mount Seymour Trail now descends, traversing a steep, rocky slope that requires some attention. Reach a tight col and resume climbing, now on exposed ledge and rock, reaching the wide, open third summit of Mount Seymour at 1449 m (4754 feet). The views are spectacular: Indian Arm, straight below; the impressive Mounts Judge Howay, Robie Reid, Baker, Shuksan, and Garibaldi; and the Howe Crest, the Strait of Georgia, and Vancouver Island. Plus a whole lot of shimmering Vancouver, Burnaby, New Westminster, and Surrey skyscrapers.

GO FARTHER

Extend your hike (or consider this as an easier option) by heading 2.1 km (1.3 miles) with little elevation gain to Dog Mountain via the First Lake Trail. Enjoy excellent views of Vancouver from Dog's summit ledges. Then return 2.4 km (1.5 miles) via the Dog Mountain Trail through beautiful old-growth forest groves. The 2.4-km (1.5-mile) Dinkey Peak Loop offers some decent views for little effort. Or traverse ski slopes to reach Goldie and Flower Lakes for an easy 3-km (1.9-mile) loop. Mystery Lake requires a little more effort, but it's still a fairly easy hike and only 2.3 km (1.4 miles) roundtrip. If you can arrange for a shuttle, hike the Old Buck Trail downhill for 5.5 km (3.4 miles).

Next page: Autumn foliage at Kanaka Creek Regional Park (Trail 32)

EASTERN MUNICIPALITIES

East of Burnaby and Burrard Inlet and north of the Fraser River are several diverse Metro Vancouver Regional District municipalities. The Tri-Cities consists of Port Moody (population 40,000), Coquitlam (population 175,000), and Port Coquitlam (population 70,000)—along with the two tiny villages of Anmore and Belcarra.

Port Moody is named for Colonel Richard Moody, the first lieutenant governor of British Columbia, and is one of the oldest non-Native settlements in the Lower Mainland. Coquitlam is BC's sixth-largest city, and like most of the district, has a diverse population. Port Coquitlam (PoCo) once consisted of large tracts of farmland, since replaced by suburban housing units. The Tri-Cities are home to large regional parks and an extensive trail network, including the Traboulay PoCo Trail, which completely encircles the city of Port Coquitlam.

Farther east is Pitt Meadows (population 22,000), named for British Prime Minister William Pitt the Younger. Located along the confluence of the Pitt and Fraser Rivers, Dutch settlers in the 1940s reclaimed much of the floodplain here for farming. Today, 86 percent of Pitt Meadows is protected farmland.

Maple Ridge (population 100,000) is BC's fifth-oldest municipality and has many historical neighborhoods. Located along the north bank of the Fraser River and at the base of the iconic Golden Ears mountain group, Maple Ridge's population has exploded since the Golden Ears Bridge linked it to Langley and the Trans-Canada Highway in 2009. Pitt Meadows and Maple Ridge both contain large regional parks and municipal trail networks. Sprawling Golden Ears Provincial Park (out of this book's scope) abuts the city and offers extensive backcountry hiking

PORT MOODY

27 təmtəmíxʷtən/ Belcarra Regional Park

DISTANCE:	More than 26 km (16 miles) of trails
ELEVATION GAIN:	Up to 575 m (1890 feet)
HIGH POINT:	558 m (1830 feet)
DIFFICULTY:	Easy to difficult
FITNESS:	Walkers, runners, hikers
FAMILY-FRIENDLY:	Yes
DOG-FRIENDLY:	On leash
AMENITIES:	Washrooms, water, picnic tables and shelters, beach, seasonal concessions, interpretive signs, historical sites
CONTACT/MAPS:	Metro Vancouver Regional Parks
BEFORE YOU GO:	Open 7 AM to dusk. The park is extremely popular, especially during the summer.
GPS:	N49.323 W122.885

GETTING THERE

Map to: Belcarra Picnic Area, Port Moody, BC. **Transit:** TransLink buses 158, 180, 182. **Parking:** Park in the Sasamat Lake parking area at White Pine Beach, or at the Belcarra Regional Park picnic area. Parking fee from 10 AM to closing from April 1 to September 30. Parking lots fill early and there is no street parking.

Occupying a rugged peninsula where Burrard Inlet yields to Port Moody and Indian Arm, təmtəmíxʷtən/Belcarra Regional Park protects more than 1100 ha (2700 acres) of stunning landscapes. On an excellent trail system, explore tidal pools, shoreline cliffs, secluded beaches, a wildlife-rich swamp, stately coniferous forests, a high ridge, and a large, inviting lake. And savor sublime views up the Indian Arm fjord, flanked by steep, imposing mountains.

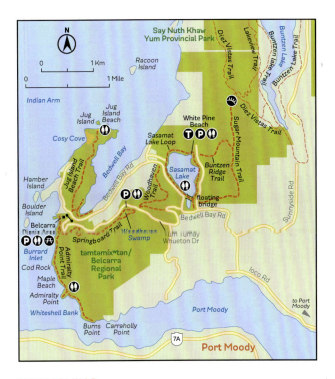

GET MOVING

Originally named after the small and isolated village of Belcarra (the least populated of the twenty-one regional district municipalities with 700 residents), in 2021 the park's name changed to include təmtəmíxʷtən (pronounced *tum-tum-waya-ten*), which means "big land (or place) for the people" in the Halkomelem language. Təmtəmíxʷtən was the largest village of the Tsleil-Waututh Nation. Along with recognizing the park as Tsleil-Waututh's ancestral land, təmtəmíxʷtən/Belcarra will now be co-managed by the First Nation and Metro Vancouver.

While ultra runners may want to take a crack at covering all of the park's trails in one swoop, most visitors will opt to

Tidal pool on Bedwell Bay

do shorter day hikes across multiple visits. The park offers some great day-hiking options of varying distances and difficulties. Consider the following:

Sasamat Lake

Most of the park's million-plus annual visitors flock to Sasamat Lake's beaches. The lake is one of the warmest bodies of waters in the Lower Mainland. The trail around the lake can be busy—especially the stretch over a 160-m (525-foot) floating bridge, which bustles with partying teens on summer days. Plan to do this wonderful, easy 3.2-km (2-mile) hike around the lake in the offseason. Sasamat is believed to be the original Indigenous name for either Burrard Inlet or Indian Arm, translating as "cool place."

Woodhaven Swamp

This easy 1.2-km (0.8-mile) loop travels around a drowned forest with good birding and wildlife-watching. While you can access this loop from a parking lot off Tum Tumay Whueton

Drive, you can make it a longer hike by following the lightly hiked 2-km (1.2-mile) Woodhaven Trail from the Sasamat Lake Loop. The trail follows along Windermere Creek before steeply climbing via lots of steps up a ridge shrouded in tall, open timber that can be eerie on a cloudy winter day.

Admiralty Point Trail
One of the more scenic trails in the park, this path travels for 3 km (1.9 miles) along rugged Burrard Inlet shoreline, ending at a ledge granting good views of Burnaby Mountain and Port Moody. The path traverses groves of towering firs and includes some ups and downs over rocky stretches. It accesses secluded, cobbled Maple Beach—as well as spurs to Cod Rock and Admiralty Point, granting excellent views of Mount Seymour, Grouse Mountain, and the Ironworkers Memorial Bridge across the inlet. Much of the way is through land that was originally set aside as a naval reserve but is now managed by Parks Canada.

Bedwell Bay Trail
This short, easy 2.3-km (1.4-mile) roundtrip trail forms a horseshoe along the tip of Bedwell Bay. The northern leg grants access to a large, rocky reef that can be explored at low tide. Views are excellent of the bay, with its rocky shoreline and mudflats and its surrounding forested hills.

Jug Island Beach Trail
Follow this moderately difficult, 2.7-km (1.7-mile) trail, climbing with the aid of steps, along and up and down a rugged ridge. Traverse some ledges before steeply descending on rough trail to remote Jug Island Beach at the tip of a small peninsula. Little Jug Island lies a short distance offshore. Savor sweeping views up Indian Arm to towering, craggy peaks. During low tide, explore (with care) fascinating tidal pools and shoreline shelves.

Springboard Trail

Take this open-to-bikes trail, climbing a ridge through attractive, quiet forest for a 2.4-km (1.5-mile) hike from Belcarra Bay to Woodhaven Swamp.

Sugar Mountain

For a challenging hike or run, follow Sugar Mountain Trail from the Sasamat Lake Loop to a viewpoint high on Sugar Mountain, looking down on Sasamat Lake and Indian Arm below. You can return via the Buntzen Ridge Trail for a 6.4-km (4-mile) loop.

GO FARTHER

Strong hikers can continue from the Sugar Mountain Trail, heading north on Diez Vistas Trail to the park's high point on Cima Amanecer (Sunrise Hill) and beyond into Say Nuth Khaw Yum (Indian Arm Provincial Park). At BC Hydro's adjacent Buntzen Lake Recreation Area, you can access many more kilometers of trails, including the popular 10-km (6.2-mile) loop around Buntzen Lake, with its floating and suspension bridges.

COQUITLAM

28 Mundy Park

DISTANCE:	16 km (10 miles) of trails
ELEVATION GAIN:	Up to 60 m (200 feet)
HIGH POINT:	175 m (575 feet)
DIFFICULTY:	Easy
FITNESS:	Walkers, runners, hikers, bicyclists
FAMILY-FRIENDLY:	Yes, and several trails wheelchair- and jogging stroller–accessible

DOG-FRIENDLY:	Both off- and on-leash trails; dogs prohibited on Nature Interpretive Trail
AMENITIES:	Washrooms, water, picnic tables and shelter, playground, sports fields, pool
CONTACT/MAPS:	Coquitlam Parks, Recreation, Culture and Facilities
BEFORE YOU GO:	Open 7 AM to dusk; park prone to flooding, prompting closures
GPS:	N49.255 W122.834

GETTING THERE

Map to: Mundy Park Hillcrest Parking Lot, Coquitlam, BC. **Transit:** TransLink buses 151, 152, 153, 156. **Parking:** Park at the Mundy Park Hillcrest Parking Lot. Additional parking at the Mundy Park East Parking Lot on Mariner Way.

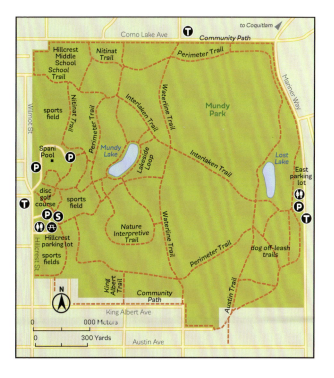

Saunter through an impressive second-growth temperate rainforest and wander along the shores of two small lakes in this large urban park in British Columbia's sixth-largest city. Most of Mundy Park's 178 ha (440 acres) are managed in a natural state and are traversed by an excellent network of trails. The park is home to endangered western painted turtles, deer, and the occasional bear.

GET MOVING

Popular with dog hikers and runners, Mundy Park allots a lot of terrain to leash-free travel. Some of the trails, however, require leashes at certain times of day—and some don't allow dogs at all. None of this seems to matter, though, to many park users, so be prepared to encounter loose dogs at this lovely park. With that said, most of the dogs you'll encounter will be well-behaved (as they should be).

Wet day at Mundy Park's temperate rainforest

The park's trail system is well-built and well-marked. Choose from several loops, or combine trails for a long run or hike. Along the park's western periphery are developed facilities such as sports fields, picnic shelters, and one of the best playgrounds around. Kids will really like the mini tree walk and all the animal sculptures.

The paved Community Path runs 5.5 km (3.4 miles) along the periphery of the park, tying together many trails, passing through the east parking lot on Mariner Way, and connecting to the off-leash dog trails and off-leash fenced area. A portion of the southern stretch of the loop uses quiet neighborhood roads.

The 4-km (2.5-mile) Perimeter Trail is very popular and scenic, traveling through attractive, century-old second-growth forest. The trail passes along little Lost Lake, which provides important habitat for a population of endangered western painted turtles. The terrain is pretty gentle, with a couple of short inclines and declines. The 1-km (0.6-mile) Nature Interpretive Trail and 1.1-km (0.7-mile) Lakeside Loop (both closed to dogs) are really pretty. Combine them for a walk in the wild, passing through impressive forest groves, crossing gurgling creeks, and encircling Mundy Lake, which sits in the center of the park.

The 1.1-km (0.7-mile) Interlaken Trail traverses the park from east to west, tying together the park's two small lakes. The 1.3-km (0.8-mile) Waterline Trail utilizes a dirt service road to traverse the park from north to south. The 0.8-km (0.5-mile) Nitinat Trail branches off the Perimeter Trail and offers a less traveled route. Nitinat (Nitinaht) is the former name of the Ditidaht, a First Nations people who reside along the west coast of Vancouver Island. I am not sure why this trail was named after them.

If you have a bout of déjà vu while traipsing through this park, blame Hollywood. The TV series *Supernatural* and the movie *Deck the Halls* both include scenes shot here.

29 Ƛ́éxətəm Regional Park (Colony Farm)

DISTANCE:	11.8 km (7.3 miles) of trails
ELEVATION GAIN:	Up to 18 m (60 feet)
HIGH POINT:	18 m (60 feet)
DIFFICULTY:	Easy
FITNESS:	Walkers, runners, hikers, bicyclists
FAMILY-FRIENDLY:	Yes, and several trails wheelchair- and jogging stroller–accessible
DOG-FRIENDLY:	On leash
AMENITIES:	Washrooms, water, picnic tables, interpretive displays, community garden
CONTACT/MAPS:	Metro Vancouver Regional Parks
BEFORE YOU GO:	Open 7 AM to dusk
GPS:	N49.297 W122.700

GETTING THERE

Map to: Coquitlam 1, Kwikwetlem First Nation, BC. **Transit:** TransLink buses 159, 169, 791. **Parking:** Park off Ƛ́éxətəm Road (also known as Colony Farm Road) in the large lot on the left at the main entrance. Alternative parking on Ƛ́éxətəm Road near Mundy Creek trailhead and on Shaughnessy Street.

Wander along the Coquitlam River through riparian forest and sprawling meadows that were once part of one of the most productive farms in the province. More than two hundred species of birds have been recorded here, at the confluence of the Coquitlam and Fraser Rivers. Alongside its excellent wildlife habitat, Ƛ́éxətəm Regional Park preserves remnants of its farming history. And the park's open fields grant excellent views of the majestic Port Mann Bridge and an emerald backdrop composed of Mount Burke and adjacent peaks.

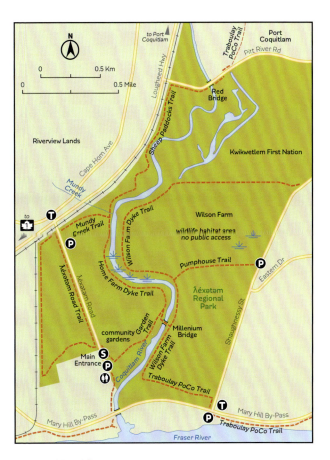

GET MOVING

ƛ̓éxətəm (pronounced *tla-hut-um*) means "to be invited" in the Halkomelem language spoken by the area's Indigenous people, the Kwikwetlem First Nation (from which Coquitlam is named).

Until July 1, 2020, this park was known as the Colony Farm. Established in 1910 to provide food for the adjacent Riverview Hospital mental health complex, the farm was once one of the most productive in British Columbia. Largely a dairy and livestock farm, it ceased operations in 1983. In 2012, Riverview closed its doors. Portions of the 405-ha (1000-acre) hospital complex and farm were subsequently sold off for subdivision, but 260 ha (642 acres) were retained as a regional park. The Kwikwetlem people have installed interpretive signs in the park, highlighting their history, culture, and connection to their ancestral land.

From the main entrance, set out through the community gardens on the Garden Trail, coming to the Millennium Bridge in 0.8 km (0.5 mile). Cross the bridge, which spans the Coquitlam River, to the Wilson Farm Dyke Trail. Follow the trail right, walking south along the river and skirting a large field. It then bends left to become the Traboulay PoCo Trail, passing an impressive cottonwood grove before reaching Shaughnessy Street in 1 km (0.6 mile).

North from Millennium Bridge, the Wilson Farm Dyke Trail reaches a junction with the Pumphouse Trail in 0.5 km (0.3 mile). The Pumphouse Trail travels 0.7 km (0.4 mile) east to the Shaughnessy Street trailhead, passing marshes and a wetland pool teeming with birds. The Wilson Farm Dyke Trail continues north along the Coquitlam River for 1.3 km (0.8 mile) before turning right to traverse flat former farmlands before making a short, steep climb to Shaughnessy Street in 1.1 km (0.7 mile). You can walk the road south 0.7 km (0.4 mile) to the Pumphouse Trail for a loop.

On the west side of the river at the Millennium Bridge, the Home Farm Dyke Trail follows the river north through former farmlands (now marshy meadows), reaching a junction in 1.1 km (0.7 mile). Here the Sheep Paddocks Trail crosses Mundy Creek and continues along the river through riparian forest and restored habitat, reaching Pitt River Road in 1.3 km (0.8 mile). It's a nice stretch of trail, and you get some good views of the Riverview complex's old buildings.

Walking along the Home Farm Dyke Trail

From the Home Farm Dyke/Sheep Paddocks Trail junction, the Mundy Creek Trail heads left, shaded by chestnuts and elms. They're remnants of the province's first arboretum, which was established on the hospital grounds in 1911. The trail comes to a trailhead on the access road in 0.4 km (0.25 mile). You can then return to the main entrance trailhead on the 1.2-km (0.75-mile) x̌éxətəm Road Trail, which parallels the road.

GO FARTHER

From the end of x̌éxətəm Road, follow a trail for 1.5 km (0.9 mile) to Maquabeak Park on the Fraser River and an excellent, close-up view of the Port Mann Bridge. For a grand adventure, follow the Traboulay PoCo Trail for a 25-km (15.5-mile) loop around Port Coquitlam. This paved and gravel trail connects parks, greenbelts, the Hyde Creek Nature Reserve, and city neighborhoods, at times traveling along the Coquitlam and Pitt Rivers.

30 Minnekhada Regional Park

DISTANCE:	10.2 km (6.3 miles) of trails
ELEVATION GAIN:	Up to 245 m (810 feet)
HIGH POINT:	175 m (580 feet)
DIFFICULTY:	Easy to moderate
FITNESS:	Walkers, runners, hikers
FAMILY-FRIENDLY:	Yes, and some trails wheelchair-accessible
DOG-FRIENDLY:	On leash
AMENITIES:	Washrooms, water, picnic tables, historic lodge
CONTACT/MAPS:	Metro Vancouver Regional Parks
BEFORE YOU GO:	Open 7 AM to dusk. Expect some recent fire damage on the High Knoll Trail; respect any closures.
GPS:	N49.297 W122.700

GETTING THERE

Map to: Minnekhada Lodge, Coquitlam, BC. **Parking:** Park at the Minnekhada Lodge. Alternative parking and trailhead at the Quarry Road Entrance, accessed from Victoria Drive off Coast Meridian Road.

A former hunting retreat from the 1930s, Minnekhada's surroundings remain rural. Wildlife flourishes here, including a myriad of birds, threatened turtles, and the occasional black bear. Wander through mature forest and around marshes bursting with birdsong and the choruses of thousands of toads. And amble up a couple of knolls providing sweeping views of the Pitt River, its extensive floodplain marshes, and the iconic Golden Ears hovering above.

GET MOVING

Starting out as a farm in 1895, Minnekhada (which means "rattling water" in the Sioux language) was given its name by its second owner, a native of Minnesota. In 1934, industrialist

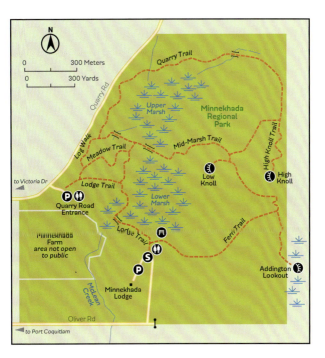

and popular Lieutenant Governor Eric Hamber bought the property to raise horses and use it as a hunting and country retreat. The population of Coquitlam was then only about 7000. His elegant, Tudor-style lodge was completed in 1937 and hosted many dignitaries, business leaders, and government officials. In 1981, a large part of the retreat became a park, and a portion of the historic farm was added in 1995, bringing Minnekhada's total area to 211 ha (521 acres).

Before or after hitting the trail, definitely check out the lodge grounds. The lodge itself is usually open to the public on Sunday afternoons. The 46 ha (114 acres) of farm grounds in the park are currently closed to the public. Two trails take off from the lodge trailhead. The Lodge Trail heads northwest for 0.9 km (0.5 mile) to the Quarry Road trailhead. The Fern

Hiking along the Lower Marsh

Trail takes off northeast for the park's knoll lookouts. It's 1.3 km (0.8 mile) to the Addington Lookout, with its view over the Pitt-Addington Marsh on the Pitt River's sprawling flood-plain. Views are good, too, out to Port Mann Bridge and the Surrey skyline. It's also 1.3 km (0.8 mile) to Low Knoll, with its excellent views of the park's wildlife-rich Lower and Upper Marshes.

Follow the Lodge Trail west to the Lower Marsh, hiking along boardwalks and elevated tread near its outlet dam on McLean Creek. In late spring and early summer, the marsh is alive with a cacophony of bird, amphibian, and insect noises. And watch your step for the tens of thousands of toadlets that emerge from the marsh during this period. Western toads are threatened throughout the province—but they are prolific here, thanks to the park's exceptional protected habitat.

Look, too, for western painted turtles, which also thrive here in the park but are threatened in the province. Continue along the Lower Marsh and veer right at a junction, coming to the Meadow Trail (which leads to the Quarry Road trailhead) and the Log Walk (which leads to the Quarry Trail and the Mid-Marsh Trail). The Mid-Marsh Trail follows a dyke between the Upper and Lower Marshes, providing lots of sublime scenery and nature-watching opportunities. The trail then climbs to meet the Quarry Trail and Fern Trail near the Low Knoll lookout. You can make a 2.8-km (1.7-mile) loop by joining the Mid-Marsh Trail with the Lodge and Fern Trails.

For a grand loop, skip the Mid-Marsh Trail and instead follow the Quarry Trail clockwise along the Upper Marsh and then ascend a ridge through attractive coniferous forest to the Fern Trail. Don't skip the 0.5-km (0.3-mile) side trail to High Knoll, with its excellent views of the Pitt River and floodplain marshes, plus peaks near and far (including Mount Baker). This loop, with the High Knoll side trip, tallies in at 5.2 km (3.2 miles). Add both the Addington Lookout and Low Knoll side trips to the mix for a hike of 6.4 km (4 miles).

PITT MEADOWS

31 Pitt River Regional Greenway

DISTANCE:	11.3 km (7 miles) of trails
ELEVATION GAIN:	Minimal
HIGH POINT:	8 m (25 feet)
DIFFICULTY:	Easy
FITNESS:	Walkers, runners, hikers, bicyclists
FAMILY-FRIENDLY:	Yes
DOG-FRIENDLY:	On leash
AMENITIES:	Washrooms, interpretive signs, picnic tables
CONTACT/MAPS:	Metro Vancouver Regional Parks
BEFORE YOU GO:	Open 7 AM to dusk. Greenway passes through active agricultural area; farm vehicles have right-of-way.
GPS:	N49.204 W122.689

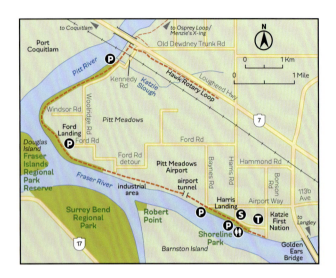

GETTING THERE

Map to: Harris Landing (Harris Road & Fraser Way), Pitt Meadows, BC. **Transit:** TransLink buses 719, 722 stop on Bonson Way near Shoreline Park trailhead. **Parking:** At the end of Harris Road, park on the roadside at the entrance to Pitt River Regional Greenway.

Hike, walk, or run along a dyke at the confluence of the Fraser and Pitt Rivers. Travel through towering cottonwood and cedar groves. Traverse farms and cranberry bogs. Enjoy views of the majestic Golden Ears Bridge and the iconic Golden Ears peaks hovering over a sprawling floodplain of farmlands. Admire undeveloped riverfronts and islands as you enjoy a pastoral *passeggiata* just minutes from bustling cities.

GET MOVING

While most of Metro Vancouver Regional District's communities continue to urbanize, Pitt Meadows still retains a primarily agricultural setting. Located on rich, large floodplains,

Pitt Meadows is better served growing produce than producing urban growth. More than 80 percent of the municipality's land base is protected farmland covered under the province's Agricultural Land Reserve program.

From the trailhead at Harris Landing, access the main Pitt River Regional Greenway trail, which is part of the Trans Canada Trail and Canyon to Coast Trail systems. To the east, the trail comes to a junction with a 1.3-km (0.8-mile) hiker-only trail that travels through cedar groves along the Fraser riverfront. There are excellent views of Barnston Island (see Trail 43) along the way. The hiker-only trail reconnects with the main trail and can be used to make a short loop.

The main trail continues east, leaving the Greenway and passing through Pitt Meadow's Shoreline Park in the Osprey Village neighborhood. The trail continues along the Fraser River through manicured lawns, passing benches and an observation deck that grants excellent views of the Golden Ears Bridge. At 1 km (0.6 mile) from Harris Landing, the trail terminates at Bonson Road.

Westward from Harris Landing, the main trail reaches the hiker-only trail in 0.8 km (0.5 mile). It then passes a spur along a canal and then the Pitt Meadows Regional Airport, with its nine flight-training schools, three helipads, and a float plane dock on the Fraser River. The trail dips under an airport connector road and then passes a runway and blueberry fields. At 2.9 km (1.8 miles) from Harris Landing, it briefly uses a road near a busy sawmill (use caution). It then resumes its way on the dyke and enters a lovely rural zone composed of farms and a forested river corridor.

The way soon bends northwest and passes through Ford Landing (parking available on Ford Road), skirting blueberry farms and cranberry bogs along the way. Marvel at the Golden Ears in the distance. Although it was originally named Golden Eyries, the word "Eyries" somehow corrupted into "Ears"—which seems appropriate for this double-peaked

The Pitt River Greenway passes by cranberry bogs on the Hawk Rotary Loop.

mountain. Enjoy views of undeveloped Douglas Island, part of the Fraser Islands Regional Park Reserve. Then bend northeast to follow the Pitt River. Benches along the way invite weary bodies to take a break.

At 8.7 km (5.4 miles), cross Katzie Slough (parking available on Kennedy Road) and continue northeast, passing cottonwoods on the left and farms on the right. Soon afterward, the trail crosses a rail line and comes to Ferry Slip Road—where ferries plied the Pitt River before the first bridge was built in 1915. At 9.5 km (5.9 miles), the Greenway comes to its end at the busy Pitt River Bridge.

GO FARTHER

You can continue beyond the bridge on the South Alouette River Dyke Trail, first along Pitt River and then Alouette River, for 10.6 km (6.6 miles). You can also loop back to Harris Landing, following a paved bike path along BC 7 (Lougheed Highway) to Harris Road in Pitt Meadows's center. Then walk sidewalks along Harris Road, passing historical buildings and new development before returning to Harris Landing. The entire 15.7-km (9.8-mile) loop is signed the Hawk Rotary Loop. It's one of several designated bike routes in the city.

32 Kanaka Creek Regional Park

DISTANCE:	11.8 km (7.3 miles) of trails
ELEVATION GAIN:	Up to 152 m (500 feet)
HIGH POINT:	108 m (350 feet)
DIFFICULTY:	Easy to moderate
FITNESS:	Walkers, runners, hikers
FAMILY-FRIENDLY:	Yes
DOG-FRIENDLY:	On leash
AMENITIES:	Washrooms, interpretive signs, picnic tables, stewardship center, hatchery, equestrian trails
CONTACT/MAPS:	Metro Vancouver Regional Parks
BEFORE YOU GO:	Open 7 AM to dusk
GPS:	N49.211 W122.510

GETTING THERE

Map to: Bell-Irving Hatchery Parking, Maple Ridge, BC. **Parking:** Park in the fish hatchery parking lot.

Wander through a greenbelt of lush forests of towering cottonwoods, mossy hemlocks, showy maples, and impressive cedars along a salmon-rearing creek in booming Maple Ridge. Hike along and into a deep ravine and admire a series of falls over well-worn sandstone cliffs.

GET MOVING

Kanaka Creek Regional Park protects 400 linear ha (988 acres) along 12 km (7.5 miles) of Kanaka Creek. An envisioned trail that would run through the entire greenbelt has not yet materialized. The Cliff Falls and Canyon area currently has the biggest trail network in the park, while the Fraser Riverfront area has a good trail system through prime riparian habitat. The creek takes its name from the Kanakas (native Hawaiians) who settled (many with First Nations wives) in

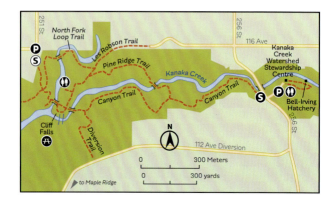

the 1830s at the mouth of the creek. Many of these Kanakas were employed by Hudson's Bay Company at Fort Langley across the Fraser River and worked in the fur brigades.

From the parking area off 256 Street, a 0.3-km (0.2-mile) interpretive trail loops through the Kanaka Creek Watershed Stewardship Centre and Bell-Irving Hatchery. Across 256 Street, find the trailhead for the 1.3-km (0.8-mile) Canyon Trail. Follow this beautiful trail downstream along the creek through gorgeous mature forest. Then climb as the creek enters a narrow sandstone canyon. At 0.6 km (0.4 mile), the Pine Ridge Trail takes off right. From here, you can choose which trail to take to Cliff Falls. The Canyon Trail continues left along the forested canyon rim, high above the creek, before descending and crossing the creek on a high bridge above the falls. The 0.6-km (0.4-mile) Pine Ridge Trail steeply drops via steps into the canyon, then crosses the creek and climbs back out, coming to the North Fork Loop Trail. Head left for 0.3 km (0.2 mile) to meet back up with the Canyon Trail at a picnic area above Cliff Falls.

A short trail heads to the rim of the canyon above the falls, but it doesn't provide good views of the main cascades. There are, however, some good views of small cascades tumbling over the well-eroded sandstone cliffs. The 1.1-km

Fall is an excellent time to visit Kanaka Creek.

(0.7-mile) North Fork Loop Trail crosses the North Fork of Kanaka Creek on two bridges (one high above a waterfall plummeting into the canyon) and traverses pretty forest groves along the North Fork. It also provides access to the Cliff Park trailhead (alternative start) on 251 Street. The short Diversion Trail leads to 112 Avenue Diversion and will give you a little workout, while the short Les Robson Trail is primarily used by area equestrians.

GO FARTHER

The Fraser Riverfront section of the park lies several kilometers west of Cliff Falls and Canyon area. To reach it, map to Kanaka Regional Park Fraser Waterfront or take TransLink 746 (flag stop) or 748 from nearby Tamarack Lane. Follow the trail along a dyke to a viewing tower that looks out over the wildlife-rich marshland. Continue to the Nature Trail, crossing Kanaka Creek and making a loop on rich floodplain through a forest of dogwoods, hazelnuts, alders, and towering cottonwoods. A few picnic tables and river viewpoints invite lingering.

Next page: *Gulls roost on snowy Boundary Bay (Trail 41).*

RICHMOND & DELTA

Richmond is the fourth-largest city in British Columbia. Nearly three-quarters of its population of 235,000 is of Asian descent, making it the largest Asian-majority city in North America. A thriving city and home to Vancouver International Airport, nearly 40 percent of Richmond's land is agricultural and produces almost half of BC's cranberry harvest.

Richmond's land base is made up of islands in the Fraser River delta, with most of the city lying on Lulu Island. The entire city is nearly at sea level and is protected from flooding by a system of dykes, many of which have been incorporated into the city's extensive trail network. Trails in Richmond run along the city's coastline and through its historical fishing village of Steveston.

True to its name, the city of Delta (population 120,000) sits on the Fraser River delta and is bordered by water on three sides: the Fraser River, the Strait of Georgia, and Boundary Bay. Much of Delta consists of floodplain and coastal flats, with half of the city's land base agricultural. Delta's Burns Bog is one of the largest undeveloped urban land masses in Canada. The city's Tsawwassen neighborhood lies in a rain shadow. Delta's parks and trails are birding hot spots during migrations.

Ancestral home of the Tsawwassen First Nation, Point Roberts (Point Bob to locals) occupies the five square mile southern tip of the Tsawwassen Peninsula. An enclave of the United States, Canadian citizens make up a good portion of the community's population of 1200, which quadruples during the summer.

RICHMOND

33 Iona Beach Regional Park

DISTANCE:	About 9 km (5.6 miles) of trails
ELEVATION GAIN:	Minimal
HIGH POINT:	4.5 m (15 feet)
DIFFICULTY:	Easy
FITNESS:	Walkers, runners, hikers, bicyclists
FAMILY-FRIENDLY:	Yes
DOG-FRIENDLY:	On and off leash; prohibited on intertidal flats and South and North Pond trails
AMENITIES:	Washrooms, interpretive signs, picnic tables
CONTACT/MAPS:	Metro Vancouver Regional Parks
BEFORE YOU GO:	Open 7 AM to dusk
GPS:	N49.217 W123.212

GETTING THERE

Map to: Iona Beach Regional Park, Richmond, BC. **Parking:** Park at Iona Jetty parking area and along Ferguson Road.

Atop the Iona Jetty, walk for 4 km (2.5 miles) straight into the Strait of Georgia. Take in sweeping views of Mount Baker, North Shore peaks, Bowen Island, Vancouver Island, and the Gulf and San Juan Islands. Then explore the North Arm Jetty via a sandy shoreline abutting expansive tidal flats. And count the birds! More than three hundred species have been sighted in this important migration hot spot on the Fraser River delta.

GET MOVING

Iona was once a separate island, now attached to Sea Island (which houses Vancouver's airport) by a causeway. It's a fascinating place to explore, known for turds and birds. Okay, before you get too alarmed, know that the former is

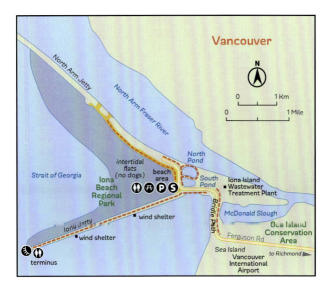

a reference to the Iona Island Wastewater Treatment Plant (not open to the public). The latter congregate, mate, and migrate on Iona's extensive tidal flats, wetlands, and dunes in prolific numbers—making this one of the best bird-watching spots not only in the Lower Mainland, but in the entire country. Aside from the countless eagles, herons, scoters, sanderlings, cormorants, hawks, and plovers, some rare species have also shown up here—including great knots, red-necked stints, and spoon-billed sandpipers.

Now about those turds—after they're treated, the effluent is piped far out to the strait via the Iona Jetty. And that jetty makes for one of the region's most interesting trails. The top of it is open to foot traffic and leashed dogs, while the lower jetty road is open to bikes and unleashed dogs. It's 4 km (2.5 miles) from the trailhead to an observation platform at the Jetty terminus. Winds can be strong on the open water. There are two wind shelters along the way (one at 1.3 km/0.8 mile and one at 2.5 km/1.6 miles) and a couple of privies too.

In addition to avian activity, expect plenty of aviation activity at Iona Beach.

You'll feel like you're hiking out in the ocean. The views across the strait in every direction are incredible.

You can also hike out on the North Arm Jetty, which is lined with log booms and provides a shipping channel on the North Arm Fraser River between Iona and the Point Grey Peninsula. The hike can be done at low tide from the beach area, following along the sandy shoreline that borders the sprawling intertidal flats between the two jetties. Pass a complex of sand dunes, rare in British Columbia. Please stay out of them. At 2.6 km (1.6 miles), come to a recent breach in the jetty (made to help restore habitat) that hinders going any farther.

North of the main parking area, a series of short trails circle a couple of ponds in a restored area. There is also access to the North Arm Fraser River. The whole area is a birding hot spot, so dogs are prohibited here. Finally, you can hike along the 1-km (0.6-mile) Bridle Path paralleling the access road to the causeway. Here you can bird-watch in McDonald Slough, an avian hot spot.

34 Richmond Nature Park

DISTANCE:	5 km (3.1 miles) of trails
ELEVATION GAIN:	Minimal
HIGH POINT:	5 m (15 feet)
DIFFICULTY:	Easy
FITNESS:	Walkers, hikers
FAMILY-FRIENDLY:	Yes, and one trail wheelchair-accessible
DOG-FRIENDLY:	Prohibited
AMENITIES:	Washrooms, interpretive signs, picnic area, playground, Nature House
CONTACT/MAPS:	City of Richmond Parks and Recreation
BEFORE YOU GO:	Open dawn to dusk; closed Sept 30, Nov 11, Dec 25, Dec 26. Nature House is admission by donation.
GPS:	N49.171 W123.094

GETTING THERE

Map to: Richmond Nature House, Richmond, BC. **Transit:** TransLink bus 40. **Parking:** Park in the lot at Richmond Nature House.

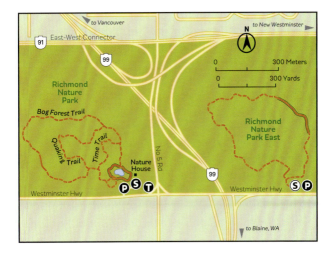

Hike on a series of short, easy loops around a small pond, across peat bogs, and through groves of shore pines and birches. The Richmond Nature Park preserves 80 ha (200 acres) of land on the eastern edge of the city's bustling commercial and residential districts. It's a window into the past, before developments and agricultural tracts covered Lulu Island.

GET MOVING

The park has two sections, separated by busy BC 99. The western section is where most folks visit, with its trail network and good infrastructure. If you're looking for the chance to commune with nature alone, the eastern section may deliver.

From the Nature House (in the western section), the 0.4-km (0.25-mile) Pond Trail takes off, passing a small garden before circling a small pond via a wide boardwalk. It's wheelchair- and jogging stroller–accessible. The Bog Forest Trail takes off from the Pond Trail—true to its name, traveling through both forest and bog. At 1.8 km (1.1 miles), it's the longest of the three loops in this section of the park. The Quaking Trail and Time Trail take off from it, offering shorter loops. Best to do them all, for about a 3.5-km (2.2-mile) total trip.

Before non-Native settlement, much of Richmond was composed of bog. A good part of the city is just 1 m (3 feet) above sea level. The Nature Park can be a saturated place. But no worries exploring here, as the trails have all been elevated and wood-chipped or built with boardwalks.

The place has a wild feel, except for the background highway and airplane noises. Look carefully at the plant life in the bog. Sphagnum moss is the defining feature, but carnivorous sundews, pitcher plants, and bladderworts all thrive in this environment. Labrador tea, bog rosemary, and western bog laurel are also profuse here, tolerating the acidic, saturated soils. These same soils have led to Richmond being a major producer of blueberries and cranberries. Pick up or download a copy of the Self-Guided Nature Walk brochure to gain a better appreciation of this environment.

After exploring the main section of Richmond Nature Park, consider heading over to the eastern section (head east on Westminster Highway for 1 km (0.6 mile), turn left on Jacombs Road, and then immediately turn left to reach the parking area and trailhead). Here find a 2-km (1.2-mile) loop with a long boardwalk stretch through more fine bog land.

Boardwalk across the bog

35 West Dyke and Middle Arm Trails

DISTANCE:	10.8 km (6.7 miles) one-way
ELEVATION GAIN:	Minimal
HIGH POINT:	6 m (20 feet)
DIFFICULTY:	Easy
FITNESS:	Walkers, hikers, runners, bicyclists
FAMILY-FRIENDLY:	Yes, and wheelchair-accessible
DOG-FRIENDLY:	On leash
AMENITIES:	Washrooms, interpretive signs, picnic area, playground
CONTACT/MAPS:	City of Richmond Parks and Recreation
BEFORE YOU GO:	Trails can be accessed from various spots
GPS:	N49.126 W123.194

GETTING THERE

Map to: Garry Point Park, Richmond, BC. **Transit:** TransLink buses 401, 402, 406, 407, 413; SkyTrain Canada Line stops at Aberdeen Station, requiring a 0.2-km (0.1-mile) walk west on Cambie Road to reach the hike's northern terminus. **Parking:** Park at Garry Point Park. Alternative parking and trailheads are located at Steveston Highway (limited), Williams Road (street), Francis Road (limited), Blundell Road (street), Westminster Highway (street), Terra Nova Rural Park, and along River Road west of No. 1 Road.

Stroll, saunter, or run along a stretch of the extensive dyke system that prevents Lulu Island from being submerged. Pass numerous historical sites, from old shipyards, canneries, and farms to the Richmond Olympic Oval. Marvel at scads of shorebirds in the Sturgeon Banks Wildlife Management Area, as well as birds of the two-engine variety taking off and touching down on Sea Island, just across the Middle Arm Fraser River. And as you explore, take in some of the best jaw-dropping sunsets in the Lower Mainland.

GET MOVING

Richmond's dykes not only help keep British Columbia's fourth-largest city from flooding, they also keep its citizens in good cardiovascular shape. Many kilometers of the city's surrounding dykes have been integrated into its large trail network. And these trails are as flat as they come, welcoming users of all ages and abilities.

Strong hikers and runners can cover the interconnecting West Dyke and Middle Arm Recreational Trails together as a 21.6-km (13.4-mile) out-and-back. But with public transportation, a one-way route is also possible. Shorter out-and-backs will suffice too, and a couple of parks along the way add even more trail options.

Starting from the West Dyke Trail's southern terminus at Garry Point Park (see Go Farther below) in the historical fishing village of Steveston, head north and pass Scotch Pond, set in offshore salt marshes. Look for ruins and remnants of the Scottish-Canadian Cannery and the Japanese-Canadian Atagi Boat Works at the pond. The trail continues northward, passing rows of well-kept houses and townhouses to the east. To the west are extensive salt marshes and mudflats, part of the 5152-ha (12,731-acre) Sturgeon Banks Wildlife Management Area. The banks support one of the country's largest concentrations of wintering shorebirds, swans, and snow geese. Bald eagles and great blue herons are prolific year-round.

At 1 km (0.6 mile), pass a small farm owned and operated by descendants of Manoah Steves, who settled Lulu Island in 1877 and for whom the village of Steveston is named. Continue north along wide salt marshes granting views out to Vancouver Island, the Gulf Islands, and Bowen Island. Wind can be fierce along this open stretch. Upon passing a washroom and side trail to Blundell Road at 3.4 km (2.1 miles), reach a golf course. Welcoming trees, including birches and oaks, line the way.

At 4.5 km (2.8 miles), a side trail takes off right for the Terra Nova Natural Area. At 5 km (3.1 miles), the trail bends west at the Westminster Highway trailhead and once again borders open salt marsh and mudflats. To the east, large, attractive trees in the Terra Nova Rural Park line the path. The trail then bends east at the mouth of the Middle Arm

West Dyke Trail along the Sturgeon Banks Wildlife Management Area

Fraser River, passing some beaches. Enjoy excellent views of Swishwash Island, Vancouver International Airport on Sea Island, and a backdrop of North Shore Mountains. At 6 km (3.7 miles), the West Dyke Trail ends near the main entrance to Terra Nova Rural Park (see Go Farther).

The Middle Arm Trail now begins, following along the Middle Arm Fraser River and River Road. Watch noisy seaplanes touch and go from a seaplane center adjacent to the airport across the river. At 7.9 km (4.9 miles), reach McCallan Road and the northern terminus of the paved Railway Greenway trail (see Go Farther). Then pass a short spur leading to an observation deck in the river, and dart under the No. 2 Road Bridge at 8.9 km (5.5 miles).

The trail, now paved, continues through a more urban environment. Pass through the Olympic Riverside Plaza at the Richmond Olympic Oval, which hosted the speed-skating events for the 2010 Winter Olympics. Then continue, passing new high-rise housing units and ducking under the Dinsmore Bridge. The trail then splits into paralleling paths, passing the John M.S. Lecky UBC Boathouse, marinas, a playground, washrooms, and benches. It reaches Cambie Road (with Sky-Train access) at 10.6 km (6.6 miles) before terminating 0.2 km (0.1 mile) farther at the Skyline Marina.

GO FARTHER

You can return via the 5.9-km (3.7-mile) Railway Greenway, first following it to the Britannia Shipyards National Historic Site (see Trail 36) and then heading west for 2 km (1.2 miles) on the Steveston Greenway trail back to Garry Point Park.

Definitely walk the 1.5-km (0.9-mile) loop through lovely Garry Point Park, a former dump site for dredged sand. The park's open landscape includes public art, interpretive signs, the Kuno Japanese Garden, the Fisherman's Memorial Needle, and jaw-dropping views from Mount Baker to Vancouver Island. Sunsets here are spectacular.

Delightful Terra Nova Rural Park (dogs prohibited) and the adjacent Terra Nova Natural Area consist of 40 ha (98 acres) of wetlands, forest, grasslands, community gardens, and a historical farmstead. Wander on more than 5 km (3 miles) of trails through the parks, which were once the site of a Musqueam village and large cannery. Check out historical buildings and let the kids go wild at the Adventure Play Environment.

36

Steveston Greenway and South Dyke Trail

DISTANCE:	7.1 km (4.4 miles) one-way
ELEVATION GAIN:	Minimal
HIGH POINT:	6 m (20 feet)
DIFFICULTY:	Easy
FITNESS:	Walkers, hikers, runners, bicyclists
FAMILY-FRIENDLY:	Yes, and wheelchair-accessible
DOG-FRIENDLY:	On leash; plus an off-leash dog park
AMENITIES:	Washrooms, interpretive signs, historical sites, picnic tables, playground
CONTACT/MAPS:	City of Richmond Parks and Recreation
BEFORE YOU GO:	Trail can be accessed from various spots
GPS:	N49.125 W123.193

GETTING THERE

Map to: Garry Point Park, Richmond, BC. **Transit:** TransLink buses 41, 401, 402, 406, 407. **Parking:** Park at Garry Point Park. Alternative parking and trailheads in Steveston on streets and municipal lots, Britannia Shipyard NHS, London Landing, No. 3 Road Fishing Pier, and at lots along Dyke Road.

Wander through the heart of Richmond's historical fishing, fish-packing, and boatbuilding village of Steveston. Then continue along the Fraser River, passing towering cottonwoods, an eloquently restored heritage farm, working farms, and sweeping views of Fraser River delta islands in the foreground of snowy Mount Baker. Reach a small slough peppered with houseboats and weathered homes on pilings, the remains of an 1880s fishing community.

GET MOVING

Long before Richmond became a cosmopolitan city, Steveston (since annexed into Richmond) was a booming fishing, boatbuilding, and cannery center. Today, it's a quaint neighborhood and tourist attraction. Its grungy past has been replaced by riverside condos, and many of its historical buildings and sites have been restored. Plan on allotting time for the multitude of interpretive signs and historical attractions along the Steveston Greenway trail. And upon your finish, plan on enjoying some of the village's gastronomical delights (particularly fish and chips).

From the Garry Point Park concession, head east on the Steveston Greenway, following along Moncton Street. Pass working docks and come to paved trail at the Gulf of Georgia Cannery National Historic Site. During the late 1800s, Steveston had more than twenty canneries, earning it the nickname "Salmonopolis." The Gulf of Georgia Cannery was the largest in British Columbia at the time, employing hundreds of workers of First Nations, Chinese, Japanese, and various European descents. Today, the site is an excellent museum and learning center.

Continue east on sidewalk along Bayview Street, passing working wharfs and catching tempting whiffs from an assortment of eateries. At 0.8 km (0.5 mile), at the intersection with No. 1 Road, pick up the paved trail and continue east, now along the South Arm Fraser River. Pass through an arch representative of the gritty canneries that once lined this stretch of river, since replaced by shiny condos and well-maintained parks and plazas. At 1.3 km (0.8 mile), come to Imperial Landing Park with its observation tower. Then cross a bridge over a lagoon (or walk on the trail around it) and pass memorials, benches, sculptures, and interpretive displays. Old pilings still stand in the tidal river, testaments to the massive BC Packers fish-packing plant that once occupied this space.

At 1.6 km (1 mile), enter the Britannia Shipyards National Historic Site, the oldest shipyard in BC. Admire its restored buildings from the 1880s. The shipyard, like the canneries, employed workers of various ethnicities, including

Imperial Landing Park

those with First Nations, European, Chinese, and Japanese backgrounds. Many lived in segregated company housing. Japanese-Canadians made up a sizable percentage of the population in Steveston during the late 1800s and early 1900s—many working as fishermen and shipbuilders. During World War II, Canada (like the United States) shamefully stripped its citizens of Japanese descent of their rights, seized their property, and relocated them to internment camps. More than 22,000 Japanese-Canadians (90 percent of Canada's Japanese-Canadian population) were interned. They weren't allowed to return to their homes until 1949. Several were deported and many relocated to Ontario. In 1988, one month after US President Ronald Reagan issued an apology and reparations to the Japanese-American community, Prime Minister Brian Mulroney followed suit for the Japanese-Canadian population.

Exiting the shipyards, the trail parallels Westwater Drive to avoid some riverside businesses. Here the Railway

Greenway trail departs north, leading 5.9 km (3.7 miles) to the Middle Arm Trail (see Trail 35). Continue east on the Steveston Greenway. At 2.1 km (1.3 miles), the trail crosses Trites Road and continues east, now paralleling Dyke Road. At 2.6 km (1.6 miles), it reaches No. 2 Road. A spur continues across the road and along farmland, connecting with a neighborhood.

The Greenway continues south on sidewalk along No. 2 Road, coming to London Landing Wharf at 3 km (1.9 mile). It now continues as the wide, graveled South Dyke Trail. Follow it, once again along the river, passing cottonwood groves, small beaches, and good views of Shady Island. At 3.5 km (2.2 miles), come to the 1880s restored London Heritage Farm. With its short trails and interpretive displays, the farm is worth a diversion.

The South Dyke Trail continues east along an agricultural zone, hugging the riverbank. Views are excellent of bird-loving Westham, Kirkland, and Duck Islands and of Mount Baker rising above them. Continue on this highly scenic stretch of trail, coming to the No. 3 Road Fishing Pier at 4.7 km (2.9 miles).

The trail continues through the No. 3 Road Bark Park, an off-leash dog park with whimsical dog cutouts. It then darts away from the river, skirting farmland and bypassing a large terminal. At 6 km (3.7 miles), it crosses Garden City Road and traverses Woodwards Slough. Finally, it returns to the riverbank and terminates at 7.1 km (4.4 miles) at Dyke Road near Finn Slough. Before returning, catch a few glimpses (while respecting private property) of this historical fishing village settled by Finnish immigrants in the 1880s.

GO FARTHER

A short, non-continuous section of the South Dyke Trail can be accessed 1.3 km (0.8 mile) east of Finn Slough. Here you can also follow the 1-km (0.6-mile) Horseshoe Slough Trail through towering cottonwoods.

DELTA

37 Deas Island Regional Park

DISTANCE:	5.9 km (3.7 miles) of trails
ELEVATION GAIN:	Minimal
HIGH POINT:	6 m (20 feet)
DIFFICULTY:	Easy
FITNESS:	Walkers, hikers, runners
FAMILY-FRIENDLY:	Yes, and several trails wheelchair- and jogging stroller–accessible
DOG-FRIENDLY:	On leash
AMENITIES:	Washrooms, interpretive signs, picnic area, historical buildings, equestrian trails
CONTACT/MAPS:	Metro Vancouver Regional Parks
BEFORE YOU GO:	Open dawn to dusk; trails prone to flooding
GPS:	N49.127 W123.058

GETTING THERE

Map to: Deas Island Regional Park, Delta, BC. **Transit:** TransLink bus 640. **Parking:** Park in Deas Island Millennium Trail parking lot on Deas Island Road, near its intersection with 62B Street.

Wander around a small island in the Fraser River teeming with birds and full of history. The island was named after John Sullivan Deas, a free Black tinsmith from South Carolina who came to British Columbia in 1862, lured by the Cariboo Gold Rush. But salmon was how Deas would make his money. Through capital provided by Captain Edward Stamp (who founded Hastings Mill, which would eventually become Vancouver), Deas founded one of the most successful canneries on the Fraser River. Follow trails to his old cannery spot, along the site of a former Greek fishing village, and to the place where Queen Elizabeth II paid tribute to the island.

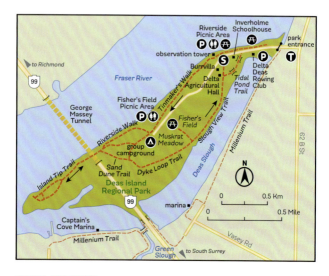

GET MOVING

Thousands of folks drive beneath Deas Island every day. This is where BC 99 enters the Massey Tunnel on its way under the South Arm of the Fraser River, connecting Delta to Richmond. The tunnel opened in 1959, putting an end to the old Ladner Ferry. Queen Elizabeth II was on hand for the dedication ceremony. You can follow the Island Tip Trail, which travels over the tunnel, to see the dedication memorial. But, alas, just as the Queen has passed, the Massey Tunnel will soon pass as well. A new, expanded tunnel, complete with bike and pedestrian lanes, is slated to open in 2030.

From the Riverside Picnic Area (a good starting point to explore the island), follow the Tinmaker's Walk (named for John Sullivan Deas) along the South Arm Fraser River. Visit the observation tower (where Deas's cannery once stood) for good views of the river, Lulu Island, Burnaby's Metrotown skyline, and North Shore peaks. Then continue downriver on the trail, coming to a group camp and several trail options. The Riverside Walk continues along the South Arm Fraser, connecting with the Island Tip Trail. The Dyke Loop Trail (shared with horses) heads to the Slough View Trail on the island's eastern side. And the Sand Dune Trail is a short jaunt over a small dune complex.

Definitely take the Island Tip Trail to the island's western tip, complete with a small beach and good views of Lulu and Kirkland Islands. For a return, follow the Dyke Loop Trail to the Slough View Trail along Deas Slough—a river channel before a causeway connected Deas to Delta. This trail is an excellent choice for bird-watching. Slough View brings you back to the Riverside Picnic Area and the short Tidal Pond Trail, which loops around a small tidal pond. It's about 5 km (3.1 miles) to loop around the island. Near the tidal pool, visit three historical buildings relocated from other parts of Delta. Check out the 1899-built Delta Agricultural Hall, the

Cottonwood trees along Deas Slough

1905-built Victorian-style home Burrvilla, and the 1909-built Inverholme Schoolhouse, one of the last one-room school-houses in Delta.

A fascinating part of Deas Island history, of which unfortunately nothing remains, was a former fishing village inhabited by Greek families. From the early 1900s to the 1950s, a series of brightly painted float homes (thirty at its height) were connected to the island by planks and pilings. Many of the families eventually relocated to nearby Ladner.

GO FARTHER

From Deas Island, follow the Millennium Trail for 2.4 km (1.5 miles) along Deas Slough to Eastpoint Park Reserve near Crescent Slough. Here, the trail splits—one arm continuing along Deas Slough for 1 km (0.6 mile) to Captain's Cove Marina, and the other heading 1.1 km (0.7 mile) along Green Slough to Admiral Boulevard near Ladner Village, with its historical homes and inviting cafés.

38 Burns Bog Delta Nature Reserve

DISTANCE:	3.2-km (2-mile) loop
ELEVATION GAIN:	Minimal
HIGH POINT:	6 m (20 feet)
DIFFICULTY:	Easy
FITNESS:	Walkers, hikers
FAMILY-FRIENDLY:	Yes
DOG-FRIENDLY:	On leash
AMENITIES:	Interpretive signs
CONTACT/MAPS:	Metro Vancouver Regional Parks
BEFORE YOU GO:	Open 7 AM to dusk. Trail prone to flooding; avoid during periods of heavy rain.
GPS:	N49.149 W122.935

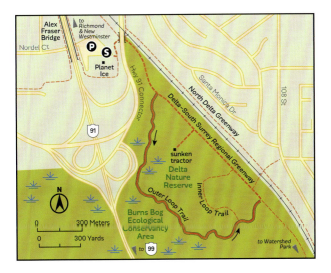

GETTING THERE

Map to: Planet Ice, Delta, BC. **Transit:** TransLink bus 640 stops at the corner of Nordel Way and Nordel Court. **Parking:** Park on the east end of the large parking lot in front of Planet Ice.

Walk a series of boardwalks on the edge of one of the largest undeveloped urban land masses in North America. The Burns Bog sprawls for more than 3240 ha (8000 acres) in the Fraser River delta. Learn about this fascinating and threatened ecosystem and its history—from First Nations berry-gathering and hunting grounds, to failed stock grounds, to peat mining, to a major conservation area classified as a wetland of international significance.

GET MOVING

From the southeast end of the parking lot, follow a paved path under Nordel Way and come to a kiosk at the entrance of the reserve. Currently 2025 ha (5000 acres) of the bog is protected as an ecological conservancy area, managed by the federal government, provincial government, regional government, and the city of Delta. Only 60 ha (148 acres) of Burns Bog is open to the public—the section separated from the conservancy area by BC 91, classified as the reserve. Be sure to visit the Burns Bog Conservation Society's website for excellent info on the bog's natural and human history.

From the entrance kiosk, walk south on the wide pathway—a section of the Delta–South Surrey Regional Greenway—following alongside Cougar Creek. The creek separates the bog from the uplands but does not flow into it. Burns is an ombrotrophic raised peat bog, receiving its water through precipitation. At 0.5 km (0.3 mile), come to a junction. You'll be returning straight, so head right on the outer loop across an extended series of boardwalks. Most of the way is treed,

The Outer Loop Trail is comprised completely of boardwalk.

but there are open stretches dominated by hardhack (spiraea), bog laurel, Labrador tea, and cotton grass.

The nature reserve consists primarily of the bog's lagg zone—the edge of the raised bog where water collects, draining from the bog and peripheral streams. Be thankful for the boardwalks. The way traverses a lovely section near BC 91, but unfortunately, vehicle noise here drowns out bird, insect, and amphibian song. Sadly, more than 70 percent of the bog has been altered through development and peat mining. During World War II, the US government purchased more than a hundred thousand bales of Burns peat to be used in firebombs.

At 1.8 km (1.1 miles), come to a junction. Here the 0.5-km (0.3-mile) Inner Loop Trail takes off left for the greenway, offering a shorter loop option—or an added bog frolic. For now, continue straight, passing big cedars and Sitka spruces and reaching the greenway at 1.9 km (1.2 miles). Turn left and follow the greenway, coming to the Inner Loop Trail again at 2.1 km (1.3 miles) and then a spur trail at 2.4 km (1.5 miles). The spur leads left for 0.2 km (0.1 mile) to a sunken tractor. Several decades ago, a thief stole a tractor, and while being pursued by the Royal Canadian Mounted Police, he drove it into a sinkhole in the bog. Attempts to retrieve the tractor have obviously been unsuccessful.

To close your loop hike, continue straight, passing the outer loop junction and returning to the trailhead at 3.2 km (2 miles).

GO FARTHER

Need more exercise? Follow the Delta–South Surrey Greenway south from its southern junction with the Outer Loop Trail. The way traverses a forested corridor along Cougar Creek, coming to the site of a peat mining operation just after passing under 72 Avenue at 1.3 km (0.8 mile). At 2.9 km (1.8 miles), it reaches 64 Avenue, where you can walk east 0.5

km (0.3 mile) to access the large Watershed Park. The park is heavily used by mountain bikers, but its wide service-road trails make for pleasant forest walks. The greenway continues south, reaching BC 10 and the south access to Watershed Park at 5.6 km (3.5 miles). At 7.4 km (4.6 miles), the greenway ends at Colebrook Road.

39 George C. Reifel Migratory Bird Sanctuary

DISTANCE:	About 4.5 km (2.8 miles) of trails
ELEVATION GAIN:	Minimal
HIGH POINT:	3 m (10 feet)
DIFFICULTY:	Easy
FITNESS:	Walkers, hikers
FAMILY-FRIENDLY:	Yes
DOG-FRIENDLY:	Prohibited
AMENITIES:	Washrooms, warming hut, picnic tables, interpretive signs, benches, bird blinds, observation tower
CONTACT/MAPS:	George C. Reifel Migratory Bird Sanctuary
BEFORE YOU GO:	Open 9 AM to 4 PM (last entry 3 PM); closed Mondays. Entry fee. Reservations required.
GPS:	N49.098 W123.179

GETTING THERE

Map to: BC Waterfowl Society, Delta, BC. **Parking:** Park in the bird sanctuary parking lot off Robertson Road.

Located on Westham Island in the Fraser River delta, the George C. Reifel Migratory Bird Sanctuary is one of the top bird-watching spots in Canada—especially in the spring and fall. During those months, millions of migratory birds pass through this lowland of tidal flats, sloughs, marshes, and

riverbanks. Lesser snow geese are prolific from November through January, while a handful of sandhill cranes reside at the refuge year-round. Be sure to pack your binoculars and bird guide.

GET MOVING

While the sanctuary is almost 300 ha (740 acres), only a small area is open to the public for hiking and walking. But that small area has nearly 4.5 km (2.8 miles) of trails and harbors thousands of birds. This is not a place to hurriedly hike through. Take your time, stopping at the bird blinds and the observation deck.

The land here, like much of Westham Island, was actively farmed throughout the last century. But since the establishment of the sanctuary in the 1960s—and the adjacent Alaksen National Wildlife Area in 1972—the Canadian Wildlife

Service, the British Columbia Waterfowl Society, and others have restored some of the land to its pre-farming state. Several of the old dykes remain in place, now acting as trails in this saturated landscape. The refuge is named for George C. Reifel, who once owned and farmed this land. His son, George H. Reifel, donated and sold the land at below-market value to the federal government, to be managed primarily as a refuge for waterfowl.

I like to hike the refuge by first covering the sanctuary's periphery, combining the East Dyke trail (along sloughs and pastures), the North Dyke (along tidal flats), the West Dyke (along tidal flats on Roberts Bank), and the SW Trail (along the Southwest Marsh). It's a 2.9-km (1.8-mile) loop. Then,

Come in winter to see snow geese take flight.

BOUNDARY BAY IBA

Pacific Northwest beer connoisseurs are well aware of IPAs. Similarly, Pacific Northwest bird-watchers are quite familiar with IBAs—Important Bird Areas. IBAs were established by BirdLife International (founded in 1922 as the International Council for Bird Protection), a global partnership of conservation groups concerned about protecting birds and their habitats. The Metro Vancouver Regional District contains four IBAs that are home to a myriad of residential species and play host to thousands of migratory birds.

More than one-and-a-half million birds pass through, stop, or reside at Boundary Bay. The 11,470-ha (28,342-acre) Boundary Bay Wildlife Management Area (which the Dyke Trail traverses; see Trail 41) is part of the larger Fraser River estuary. This estuary, with its salt flats and eelgrass beds, supports the largest wintering waterfowl and shorebird populations in Canada. Take a hike here in November and witness thousands of dunlins, western sandpipers, and black-bellied plovers. You'll probably also see brants, mallards, loons, wigeons, and herons. This area is a great place for spotting birds of prey too—watch for raptors, eagles, hawks, harriers, falcons, and snowy owls.

From November to February Boundary Bay supports a large bald eagle population, drawn down to the region from northern British Columbia, the Yukon Territory, and Alaska to feast on salmon carcasses. The Fraser River estuary supports thousands of migrating lesser snow geese from Russia's Wrangel Island—the last major breeding population in Asia. The snow geese are most apt to be spotted on Westham Island and Roberts Bank.

The best bird-watching spots in this book include Iona Beach Regional Park (Trail 33), West Dyke and Middle Arm Trails (Trail 35), Steveston Greenway and South Dyke Trail (Trail 36), Boundary Bay Regional Park (Trail 40), Boundary Bay Dyke Trail (Trail 41), Lily Point Marine Park (Trail 42), Crescent Beach and Blackie Spit (Trail 46), Serpentine Fen (Trail 50), and White Rock Promenade (Trail 51).

I walk 2.1 km (1.3 miles) on the interior trails, traveling up the Main Trail (along a slough and marsh) and circling back on the Inner Grassy Trails (along the display ponds). I then take the Auger Trail to the Cross Dyke—stopping at its viewing platform looking out over the Southwest Marsh—before heading up the Center Dyke through a tunnel of hawthorns to the observation tower (10 m/32 feet tall).

The view from the tower across the sanctuary—with its myriad fields, ponds, and sloughs—is excellent. On clear days, savor views of Mount Baker, the San Juan and Gulf Islands, and Vancouver Island across the Strait of Georgia.

I usually return to the visitor's center on the West Dyke, enjoying its sweeping views of Vancouver Island and the Gulf Islands—and in season, thousands of lesser snow geese hunkered in the tidal mudflats. These geese migrate all the way from Russia's Wrangel Island and dominate the sanctuary in winter, but nearly three hundred species of birds have been recorded here. Waterfowl are prolific year-round, especially mallards. Look for teals, mergansers, canvasbacks, avocets, hawks, and owls—including the occasional wintering snowy owl. And you'll usually get close-up views of a few residing sandhill cranes.

40 Boundary Bay Regional Park

DISTANCE:	6 km (3.7 miles) of trails
ELEVATION GAIN:	Minimal
HIGH POINT:	3 m (10 feet)
DIFFICULTY:	Easy
FITNESS:	Walkers, hikers, runners, bicyclists
FAMILY-FRIENDLY:	Yes, and some trails wheelchair-accessible
DOG-FRIENDLY:	On leash
AMENITIES:	Washrooms, water, picnic tables and shelters, interpretive signs, playground, concessions
CONTACT/MAPS:	Metro Vancouver Regional Parks
BEFORE YOU GO:	Open 7 AM to dusk. Parking fills fast during summer; plan to arrive early.
GPS:	N49.016 W123.041

GETTING THERE

Map to: Centennial Beach parking lot, Delta, BC. **Transit:** TransLink buses 601, 619. **Parking:** Park in the large Centennial Beach parking lot at the end of 6b Avenue. Alternative parking and trailhead at sports courts, 0.3 km (0.2 mile) south on 66a Street.

Despite its small size—just 19 ha (47 acres)—more than one million people visit this park each year, making it the second-busiest Metro Vancouver Regional District park. Most folks swarm Boundary Bay's sandy Centennial Beach during the summer. Many others flock here in spring and fall for bird migrations. But this park's trail system is a delight to hike, walk, or run year-round.

GET MOVING

You can make a beeline on a boardwalk right for Centennial Beach—which is what most folks do if it's summer. But the beach is great to visit in winter, too, when you can walk the wide tidal flats sans crowds. The view across Boundary Bay

Wintering brants in Boundary Bay

to Mount Baker hovering over the Semiahmoo Peninsula is simply sublime.

In addition to the boardwalk, four trails take off from the parking lot. One parallels 6b Avenue along a creek, providing a connector to the bus stop on Boundary Bay Road. The short Dune Trail makes a loop in the park's rare dune environment. Outside of the established trails, dune travel is prohibited in order to protect threatened birds and plants. The Savannah Trail leads north, skirting the park's Dr. Brink Wildlife Reserve (closed to the public); from the trail, you'll have some views into the reserve.

The Savannah Trail connects with the 12 Ave Dyke Trail (which can also be accessed from the parking area) and Raptor Trail; you can combine them to make a great little 3.2-km (2-mile) loop. The Savannah Trail continues as a boardwalk through a marsh between the two trails. Near its junction with the 12 Ave Dyke Trail, find a bird observation tower. Scan the marsh for songbirds and the bay for a plethora of birds of all types. This is one of the most important stops along the Pacific Flyway migration route, so thousands of sandpipers, dunlins, and plovers pass through here during the shorter months. Look, too, for snowy owls, short-eared owls, wigeons, teals, brants, snow geese, bald eagles, grebes, and herons.

Where the 12 Ave Dyke Trail meets back up with the Raptor Trail is another observation deck. This one overlooks the Beach Grove Lagoon and Spit (no public access), which almost always flourish with feathered visitors. From here, the 12 Ave Dyke Trail continues west 0.3 km (0.2 mile) to the 12 Avenue trailhead (limited parking). The Raptor Trail heads south, connecting to a series of short trails before traversing marsh and grasslands. Along the way, look for raptors; they are fond of this habitat because of the rodents, amphibians, and small birds it provides.

Plans are underway to construct a new Perimeter Trail, which will allow for a longer loop option.

GO FARTHER

From the 12 Ave Dyke trailhead on 12 Avenue, walk north on Beach Grove Road for 1.1 km (0.7 mile) to the Dyke Trail (see Trail 41). During low tide, you can walk Centennial Beach south for 1.1 km (0.7 mile) to the Boundary Bay border marker on the international border (but don't go any farther without clearing customs!).

41 Boundary Bay Dyke Trail

DISTANCE:	16.9 km (10.5 miles) one-way
ELEVATION GAIN:	Minimal
HIGH POINT:	3 m (10 feet)
DIFFICULTY:	Easy
FITNESS:	Walkers, hikers, runners, bicyclists
FAMILY-FRIENDLY:	Yes
DOG-FRIENDLY:	On leash; prohibited on shoreline trails in Mud Bay Park Oct 15–Apr 15
AMENITIES:	Washrooms, picnic tables, interpretive signs, equestrian trails
CONTACT/MAPS:	Metro Vancouver Regional Parks; City of Surrey Parks and Recreation
BEFORE YOU GO:	Open 7 AM to dusk. Be aware of seasonal bird hunting. Crosses active agricultural zone; expect farm machinery on the trail.
GPS:	N49.090 W122.861

GETTING THERE

Map to: Mud Bay Park, Surrey, BC. **Transit:** TransLink buses 603, 604, 614 stop at 16 Avenue in Tsawwassen, requiring a 0.2-km (0.1-mile) walk north on Beach Grove Road to Dyke Trail's western trailhead (no parking). **Parking:** Park at the lot where Railway Road meets the Mud Bay Park Loop.

Alternative trailheads and parking in Delta on 104 Street (at Delta Heritage Airpark), 72 Street, and 64 Street.

Walk on a level path along Boundary Bay's glistening mud-flats and extensive intertidal marshes beholding birds—hundreds of thousands of them! Boundary Bay bursts with migratory and wintering birds. But there's more than birds in the bay. Nearly two-thirds of the Fraser River estuary's harbor seal population lives here. Orcas frequent these waters too. Definitely pack your binoculars. And while not watching for wildlife, enjoy stunning views across the bay to the San Juan Islands and snowy volcano Mount Baker.

GET MOVING

Any section of this nearly 17-km (10.5-mile) trail will satisfy. Strong hikers and runners will have no problem completing it in its entirety. The trail starts in Surrey's Mud Bay Park, which sits on a small delta in the northeast end of Boundary Bay, fed by the Serpentine and Nicomekl Rivers. Two short shore-line trails (closed to dogs from October 15 to April 15 to protect nesting birds) diverge from the Dyke Trail, allowing for a great 2.8-km (1.7-mile) loop option. The Dyke Trail skirts the 11,470-ha (28,342-acre) Boundary Bay Wildlife Management Area, a critical Important Bird Area (see "Boundary Bay IBA" sidebar on page 203). From November through March, you'll encounter scads of folks set up with scopes. This is one of the best bird-watching areas in Canada. This area supports plenty of non-feathered species too.

Head west, at first paralleling busy BC 99—the adjacent traffic can be noisy. At 2.2 km (1.4 miles), the trail leaves Surrey for Delta and continues to run alongside Mud Bay, a smaller bay within Boundary Bay. Enjoy good views across to Crescent Beach and Blackie Spit (Trail 46) in South Surrey.

Winter sunset over Twawwassen Peninsula and Boundary Bay

And during the migration season, thousands of waders crowd the mudflats. After passing the BC 91 interchange, the trail moves away from BC 99 and birdsong replaces the highway buzz.

The trail continues along a dyke that separates salt flats and mudflats on the left from agricultural lands on the right. While Delta is home to more than 100,000 residents, half of its land base is agricultural. Farm vehicles frequently use the Dyke Trail; be sure to yield to them. And always keep your dogs under control so that they do not interfere with farming operations or sensitive bird areas.

At 6 km (3.7 miles), come to the Delta Heritage Airpark trailhead. Look out into the bay here for a large array of pilings. These are remnants of the large oyster-farming operations that were discontinued in the 1960s. The trail continues through a rural landscape along the bay; watch for shorebirds and waterfowl. Look up into overhanging tree branches for hawks and eagles. And in winter, scan the flats for snowy owls, and the fence posts for short-eared owls. Watch for coyotes in both the farm fields and the bay flats.

At 12.8 km (8 miles), come to the 72 Street trailhead. Here you can appreciate wildlife art sculptures and check out interpretive panels. At 15.1 km (9.4 miles), come to the 64 Street trailhead. The trail bends south along the bay. Enjoy good views of Mount Baker to the east, San Juan Islands to the south, and the North Shore Mountains to the north. At 16.9 km (10.5 miles), the trail ends at Beach Grove Road in Tsawwassen.

GO FARTHER

If you want to keep hiking, you can follow Beach Grove Road south through a quiet residential area for 1.1 km (0.7 mile) to Boundary Bay Regional Park (Trail 40), where there are several more miles of good trails, a lovely beach, and of course more excellent bird-watching opportunities.

POINT ROBERTS

42   Lily Point Marine Park

DISTANCE:	3.5 km (2.2 miles) of trails
ELEVATION GAIN:	Up to 70 m (220 feet)
HIGH POINT:	67 m (220 feet)
DIFFICULTY:	Easy to moderate
FITNESS:	Walkers, runners, hikers, bicyclists
FAMILY-FRIENDLY:	Yes
DOG-FRIENDLY:	On leash
AMENITIES:	Washrooms, equestrian trails
CONTACT/MAPS:	Whatcom County Parks and Recreation
BEFORE YOU GO:	Open 8 AM to dusk. Beach area may not be passable in high tides. International border crossing required.
GPS:	N48.981 W123.028

GETTING THERE

Map to: Lily Point Marine Park, Point Roberts, WA. **Parking:** Park in the lot at the end of APA Road.

Encompassing 111 ha (275 acres) of mature forest, 2.3 km (1.4 miles) of shoreline, and impressive bluffs reaching 70 m (220 feet) high, Lily Point is the crown jewel of the Tsawwassen Peninsula. Hike along the towering bluffs and down to the beach, taking in breathtaking views of Mount Baker across Boundary Bay. Watch for seals, otters, and eagles. Especially eagles—they're prolific here.

GET MOVING

While Lily Point is the largest undeveloped tract in Point Roberts, that wasn't always the case. For a long time, this was the site of an important reef net fishery run by the Cowichan, Lummi, Saanich, and Semiahmoo First Nations. When non-Native settlers arrived in the region, they too were soon

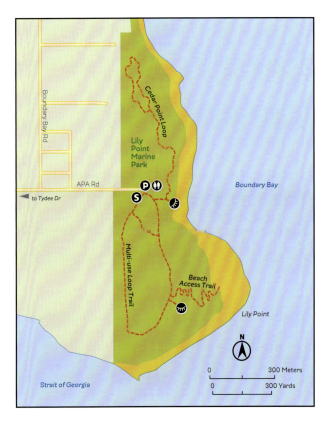

drawn to the point's abundant fish populations. From 1884 to 1917, the Alaska Packers Association (APA) operated a large salmon cannery here. All that remains of the cannery today are barnacled pilings and scattered, rusting debris. The area could have been developed into vacation homes, but instead Whatcom County acquired it in 2008—thanks to the tireless efforts of The Nature Conservancy, the Whatcom Land Trust, various Washington State agencies, and many concerned locals.

There is a nice network of trails in the park, including a forested bluff-top loop, a view-packed bluff-edge loop, and a trail leading down to Lily Point and the park's beaches. From the parking area, the 1.4-km (0.9-mile), double-track Multi-Use Loop Trail (open to bikes and horses) takes off south through a forest of mature conifers.

Going clockwise on the Multi-Use Loop, immediately reach the Cedar Point Loop that branches off to the east. Follow it for a gorgeous 1.6-km (1-mile) lollipop loop, soon coming to an incredible bluff-top view. Look directly below at Lily Point, and gaze out across Boundary Bay to the Cheam Range, Mount Baker, and a slew of North Cascades peaks. Look for eagles perched in large maples and firs. Then continue north on the trail for 0.5 km (0.3 mile) to a junction. Here a 0.6-km (0.4-mile) loop travels through big cedars and firs.

To reach Lily Point, follow the Multi-Use Loop Trail clockwise from the Cedar Point Loop junction, passing a connector trail and reaching another junction in 0.5 km (0.3 mile). Here, a 90-m (300-foot) trail leads to a bluff-top view south

A pair of juvenile bald eagles against a backdrop of snowy Mount Baker

to Lummi, Orcas, and Saturna Islands. For Lily Point, head left, descending via switchbacks into a lush ravine shaded by giant maples before reaching a grassy flat. In 0.6 km (0.4 mile), the trail reaches the beach at Lily Point. Rows of pilings from the old cannery still stand. During low tides, you can hike 0.8 km (0.5 mile) southwest on the beach beneath towering white bluffs, passing glacial erratics and a vehicle graveyard, to the park's western boundary. You can also hike north 1.3 km (0.8 mile) along the beach to the park's northern boundary, passing tidal flats, a nice swimming area (with some of the warmest salt water in Washington), and beneath more impressive bluffs.

When you're done exploring, you can take the Multi-Use Loop Trail back, looping along the park's western border and returning to the trailhead in 1 km (0.6 mile).

GO FARTHER

Point Roberts has a few other delightful places to hike. Just 2.6 km (1.6 miles) from Lily Point is Baker Field Park (access from Benson Road), with its 3.2 km (2 miles) of trails—including the whimsical Enchanted Forest Trail, complete with fairies, gnomes, and elves. In northwestern Point Roberts, find Monument Park, sitting directly on the 49th parallel (access from Roosevelt Way). Here you can follow a 0.5-km (0.3-mile) path to a beautiful stretch of undeveloped beach below a bluff and hike south along the surf for about 0.8 km (0.5 mile). And southwestern Point Roberts has lovely Lighthouse Marine Park. Here you can wander on a 0.6-km (0.4-mile) trail and explore a beautiful beach while enjoying views out to the San Juan and Gulf Islands, perhaps even catching a glimpse of a whale. Just don't go looking for any lighthouses. None were ever built on this parcel, which originally was intended to house one.

Next page: Edge Farm Trail in Derby Reach Regional Park (Trail 53)

SURREY & LANGLEY

Surrey (population 700,000) is British Columbia's second-largest city and the tenth most populated in Canada. Surrey is also BC's third-largest city in area, with a land mass that stretches from the United States border to the Fraser River. Immigration has fueled this city's explosive growth in the last few decades, making it ethnically diverse, with nearly 40 percent of its population of South Asian descent. Surrey consists of six town centers and many suburban neighborhoods, yet more than a quarter of its land base is agricultural. It's a city of parks, boasting more than eight hundred, with 450 km (280 miles) of trails.

Bordered by Surrey on three sides and facing Semiahmoo Bay is the small city of White Rock (population 22,000). A little more than a century ago, thanks to the Great Northern Railway passing through, White Rock and Surrey's Crescent Beach became popular beach resorts for folks from Vancouver and New Westminster. White Rock's promenade attracts scads of walkers from near and far.

Langley consists of a sprawling township (population 150,000)—extending from the United States border to the Fraser River—and a small municipality, the City of Langley (population 32,000). The township comprises several neighborhoods, including Fort Langley, a former Hudson's Bay Company post that led to the birth of British Columbia.

The township contains some of the Lower Mainland's richest agricultural lands, and 75 percent of its base is within the province's Agricultural Land Reserve. Many kilometers of trails traverse Langley's historical sites, Fraser River waterfront, and its large regional parks.

SURREY

43 Surrey Bend Regional Park

DISTANCE:	6.8 km (4.2 miles) of trails
ELEVATION GAIN:	Minimal
HIGH POINT:	3 m (10 feet)
DIFFICULTY:	Easy
FITNESS:	Walkers, runners, hikers, bicyclists
FAMILY-FRIENDLY:	Yes, and several trails wheelchair-accessible
DOG-FRIENDLY:	On leash
AMENITIES:	Washrooms, interpretive signs, picnic tables and shelter
CONTACT/MAPS:	Metro Vancouver Regional Parks
BEFORE YOU GO:	Open 7 AM to dusk. Park prone to flooding, prompting closures.
GPS:	N49.194 W122.729

GETTING THERE

Map to: Surrey Bend Regional Park, Surrey, BC. **Parking:** Park in the lot on Trigg Road.

Surrey Bend Regional Park is Surrey's largest park at 348 ha (860 acres), and one of its least developed. The park was opened to the public in 2015 after the provincial, regional, and municipal governments worked for two decades to secure this property and save it from industrial development. This sprawling tract of bog and riparian forest is one of the last large stretches of non-dyked shoreline on the lower Fraser River. Allowing the forces of nature to act freely, Surrey Bend is prone to flooding and shoreline shifts. Birds, amphibians, and insects (think mosquitoes) are prolific on this saturated property. And the cottonwoods are massive. Well-built trails should help keep your feet dry as you explore this remarkable park.

GET MOVING

From the parking lot, the 1.7-km (1.1-mile) Spirea Loop Trail follows two channels through birch groves and around a smaller wetland complex. It's an excellent trail for bird-watching. While Surrey Bend is a large park, about 80 percent of it is closed to the public to help protect its sprawling, ecologically sensitive bog. But the 1.5-km (0.9-mile) Pacific Trail skirts this bog along a small channel, allowing you to peer along its edges to look for some of its myriad denizens.

The 1.6-km (1-mile), hiker-only Parsons Trail travels along its namesake channel, granting good views to Barnston Island across the log-boomed water. It also offers views of the lifeline of southwest BC—the Fraser River. The highlight of this trail, however, is the massive, towering black cottonwoods. The rich alluvial soils here have favored these trees. They're prolific, gargantuan, and simply breathtaking, easily rivaling in size and girth many an old-growth conifer grove. Combine the three trails for a 4.2-km (2.6-mile) loop around the periphery of the open-to-the-public section of the park.

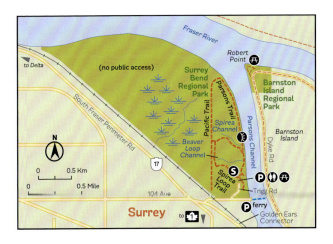

GO FARTHER

Looking for a much longer walk? From the parking lot, follow a trail 0.3 km (0.2 mile) to the Barnston Island ferry. Then walk onto the free (and on demand) ferry for a five-minute ride across Parsons Channel to 600-ha (1500-acre) Barnston Island. This level island has a population of around a hundred, consisting mostly of agricultural lands and a small Katzie First Nation reserve. The MVRD manages two small parcels on opposite ends of the island as the Barnston Island Regional Park.

From the ferry landing, walk north on the Dyke Road for 1.7 km (1.1 mile) to the Robert Point unit of the park (privy and picnic tables). Stroll on its short loop trail through towering cottonwoods to Robert Point and good views across Parsons

The Golden Ears rising behind Barnston Island

Channel to Surrey Bend. The Mann Point section of the park, on the eastern end of the island, lacks facilities. From a small, grassy area, you can enjoy excellent views of the Golden Ears Bridge and the Golden Ears peaks. You can also follow a short trail (prone to flooding) to the Fraser River. From the ferry landing, a loop around the island on the lightly driven Dyke Road is 10 km (6.2 miles). All land on the island, except for the regional park units, is private, so stay on the road. On weekends, expect lots of cyclists to be sharing the ferry and Dyke Road with you.

44 Tynehead Regional Park

DISTANCE:	15 km (9.3 miles) of trails
ELEVATION GAIN:	Up to 60 m (200 feet)
HIGH POINT:	60 m (200 feet)
DIFFICULTY:	Easy
FITNESS:	Walkers, runners, hikers, bicyclists
FAMILY-FRIENDLY:	Yes, and several trails wheelchair-accessible
DOG-FRIENDLY:	On leash, plus a leash-free zone
AMENITIES:	Washrooms, picnic tables and shelter, fish hatchery, historical structures, group camp
CONTACT/MAPS:	Metro Vancouver Regional Parks
BEFORE YOU GO:	Open 7 AM to dusk
GPS:	N49.178 W122.761

GETTING THERE

Map to: Tynehead Hatchery, Surrey, BC. **Transit:** TransLink buses 50, 388. **Parking:** Enter the park at the Tynehead Hatchery entrance and park there. Alternative trailheads with parking can be found at the Serpentine Hills entrance on 96 Avenue, the Serpentine Fields entrance on 168 Street, and the Serpentine Hollow entrance on 161 Street.

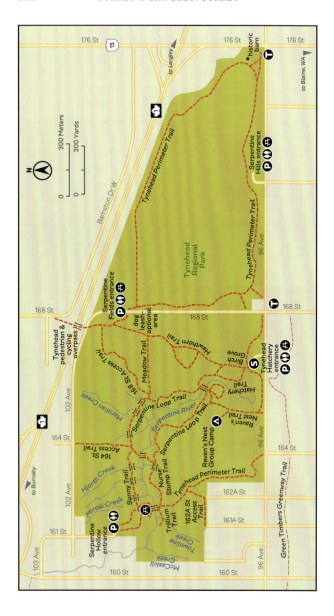

Two parks in one. Take to Tynehead's western tract and explore an excellent network of trails along the rippling, salmon-spawning Serpentine River and through groves of towering spruces, cedars, and firs. Tynehead's eastern tract invites you to go for a run or ride on a wide, paved trail across rolling terrain, with a hilltop meadow granting delightful views from Mount Baker to the Golden Ears.

GET MOVING

One of Surrey's largest and finest parks, Tynehead is named after one of the earliest non-Native settlements in the city. The park protects important habitat surrounding the head-waters of the Serpentine River. The trail system here is top-notch, with extensive riverside boardwalks, a long and paved multiuse loop, a wheelchair-accessible loop to the river via gorgeous forest groves, and a large leash-optional area. Tynehead can get busy, but with its large trail system and 260 ha (642 acres) of parkland, there's plenty of room to roam.

For a short and wheelchair-accessible route in the park's western tract, take to the Birch Grove, Hatchery, and Salmon Habitat Loop Trails. Combine these three trails for a 1.5-km (0.9-mile) route, traveling through a gorgeous grove of birches (prettier in the fall) and across the Serpentine River on a big bridge. Interpretive panels help you appreciate the river's role as a critical salmon-rearing habitat. Come in the fall for the spawn, and check out the hatchery (when gates are open) to see coho, chum, and chinook salmon.

Follow the Hatchery Trail to the Serpentine Loop Trail for a really pretty 2.4-km (1.5-mile) loop along the Serpentine River, including extensive boardwalks and two bridges that cross the river. Expand that loop by 1.1 km (0.7 mile) by skipping the second bridge across the Serpentine River, instead continuing on the Sunny Trail and returning on the Nurse Stump Trail. The lightly hiked, 0.4-km (0.25-mile) 164

St Access Trail also takes off near here, allowing access to a lovely meadow. And farther east, the 0.6-km (0.4-mile) 168 St Access Trail travels through a tunnel of hawthorns. Continue on the Sunny Trail and pass lots of fine, towering trees—including a giant old-growth Sitka spruce. Contrast the drier, northern side of the river on the Sunny Trail with the damper, lusher south side along the Nurse Stump Trail. Where this loop crosses the river, you can extend your hike with a stair climb up the 0.3-km (0.2-mile) Trillium Trail for an overlook of the rippling river.

You can also take Birch Grove to the Hawthorn Trail, which traverses the very large leash-optional area. There are lots of mud holes and open space for your dog to explore.

Serpentine Loop Trail

The eastern tract of the park, known as the Serpentine Hills, consists of a 4.5-km (2.8-mile) paved loop section of the Tynehead Perimeter Trail. This popular loop (open to bikes) rolls a little, traversing restored forest and a large meadow that houses artwork, interpretive signs, and a historical barn that was built by hand. From the meadow, take in views out to Mount Baker and the Golden Ears peaks. Access this loop by walking east from the hatchery parking lot for 0.4 km (0.25 mile) on the Tynehead Perimeter Trail.

GO FARTHER

South and adjacent to the hatchery entrance is 40-ha (98-acre) Bothwell Park, protecting a large bog along the Serpentine River. The Green Timbers Greenway trail traverses a small corner of the park. A little farther south (access from 164 Street), you can find the small but lovely Godwin Farm Biodiversity Preserve Park (dogs prohibited) with a lovely pond, big timber, and a delightful little 1.3-km (0.8-mile) trail system.

45 Green Timbers Urban Forest Park

DISTANCE:	More than 16 km (10 miles) of trails
ELEVATION GAIN:	Up to 30 m (100 feet)
HIGH POINT:	115 m (375 feet)
DIFFICULTY:	Easy
FITNESS:	Walkers, runners, hikers, bicyclists
FAMILY-FRIENDLY:	Yes
DOG-FRIENDLY:	On leash
AMENITIES:	Washrooms, picnic area, Surrey Nature Center
CONTACT/MAPS:	City of Surrey Parks and Recreation
BEFORE YOU GO:	Open dawn to dusk
GPS:	N49.178 W122.829

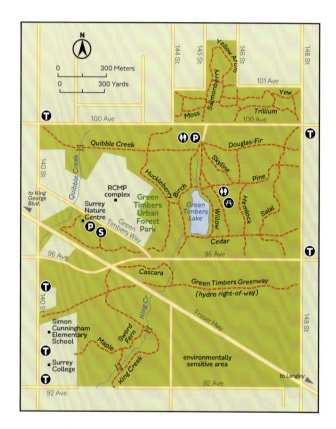

GETTING THERE

Map to: Surrey Nature Centre, Surrey, BC. **Transit:** TransLink buses 345, 395, 502, 503; SkyTrain's new Surrey Langley extension (opening in 2028) on the Expo Line will have a stop at 140 Street. **Parking:** Park at Surrey Nature Centre. Alternative parking and trailhead on 100 Avenue between 144 Street and 148 Street.

Enjoy a large dose of nature just minutes from Surrey's bustling City Centre and Guildford Town Centre. Wander on more than 16 km (10 miles) of trails in this 226-ha (560-acre) urban forest. Hike through groves of towering conifers. Amble along King Creek and stroll along the shoreline of Green Timbers Lake. And frolic across a large meadow that bustles with birds, boisterous children, and walkers of all backgrounds and abilities.

GET MOVING

A large, wonderful greenbelt in the heart of British Columbia's second-largest city, Green Timbers Urban Forest Park has a somewhat sad backstory. Once part of a more than 5000-acre tract of towering primeval forest, Green Timbers was one of the last tracts of old growth remaining on the old Pacific Highway connecting Vancouver, BC, to San Diego, California. Folks from near and far came to admire and experience this accessible ancient forest. Despite early calls to protect it and public outcry over plans to log it, it was all clear-cut by 1930.

It was, however, immediately replanted with native stock, becoming BC's first forest plantation. A forest nursery, arboretum, and education center were also established on the grounds. But over the next few decades, urban development chipped away at the forest. The nursery—which once provided stock for replanting logged areas all over the province—was supplanted by a huge Royal Canadian Mounted Police (RCMP) complex. In the 1980s, Surrey residents voted overwhelmingly to protect the remaining forest. A new nature center was opened at the old arboretum grounds, and a large addition to the forest was added in the 1990s.

Many of the park's trails are open to bicycles, but the trails are fairly wide and visibility is good. Kids will want to check out the Surrey Nature Centre. Explore some of the short trails near the center, admiring exotics and the manicured grounds. Then cross Green Timbers Way to reach the Huckleberry Trail and head north to connect with the core of the park's trails, which are well signed and maintained.

The Birch and Willow Trails are exceptionally scenic, traveling along King Creek and around Green Timbers Lake. This beautiful lake is artificial, and the rich riparian habitat feeding and draining it was reclaimed and reforested. In the late '80s, park officials cleared 17 ha (42 acres) of forest here to build sports fields. The decision prompted much public outcry, which led to its reclamation as rich wildlife habitat and the establishment of a park watchdog organization, the Green Timbers Heritage Society. From the 100 Avenue parking lot, it's about 1.6 km (1 mile) to loop around the lake.

Trails east of the lake travel through nice stands of evergreens, now approaching a hundred years old. Trails north of 100 Avenue tend to be lightly traveled. Several of them include large stretches of boardwalks traversing wetlands,

Green Timbers Lake, which was once slated to be sports fields

and the largest Douglas-fir in the park can be found along the Yew Trail. In the park's northwest corner, the 1-km (0.6-mile) Quibble Creek Trail travels past a huge glacial erratic. Trails south of Fraser Highway are also generally lightly traveled. Here you can follow the 1-km (0.6 mile) King Creek Trail on an old logging railroad bed. The paved Green Timbers Greenway trail traverses the park via a powerline swath for 1.5 km (0.9 mile). A grand hike around most of the park will register around 10 km (6.2 miles).

GO FARTHER

You can follow the paved Green Timbers Greenway from where it crosses 148 Street for 4 km (2.5 miles) east to Tynehead Regional Park (Trail 44) and Bothwell Park, with their kilometers of excellent trails.

46 Crescent Beach and Blackie Spit

DISTANCE:	About 5 km (3.2 miles) of trails
ELEVATION GAIN:	Minimal
HIGH POINT:	3 m (10 feet)
DIFFICULTY:	Easy
FITNESS:	Walkers, runners, hikers
FAMILY-FRIENDLY:	Yes
DOG-FRIENDLY:	Both on-leash and off-leash areas; prohibited on Crescent Beach May 15–Sept 15 and on Blackie Spit and its adjacent Environmental Sensitive Area
AMENITIES:	Washrooms, picnic tables, interpretive signs, community gardens
CONTACT/MAPS:	City of Surrey Parks and Recreation
BEFORE YOU GO:	Park open dawn to dusk. Parking area gated at night; note time closure.
GPS:	N49.059 W122.882

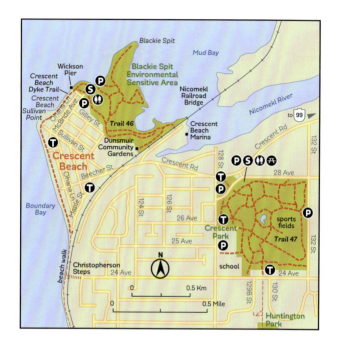

GETTING THERE

Map to: Blackie Spit Park, Surrey, BC. **Transit:** TransLink buses 350, 855. **Parking:** There are several public parking lots on McBride Avenue.

Spectacular sunsets, sprawling tidal flats, sublime views of islands and mountains, and more than three hundred species of recorded birds all make Surrey's Crescent Beach and Blackie Spit Parks choice spots for a run, walk, hike, or evening stroll. Popular summer getaway spots since the early twentieth century, these locations can get crowded. Fall and winter—when migratory birds take to the area's bays, wetlands, and marshes—are ideal times for a visit.

GET MOVING

From the large parking area, you can set out south for Crescent Beach, east for Blackie Spit Park's trails, or north for Blackie Spit itself. The spit—which juts 0.3 km (0.2 mile) into Mud Bay near the mouth of the Nicomekl River—is named after a local settler and is one of the best places in the Lower Mainland for bird-watching. Dogs are not permitted and neither is leaving the trail, due to the presence of ground-nesting birds.

An off-leash dog beach, however, is just south of the spit access trail, and a large fenced-in leash-free area is just east of the parking lot. Several short trails here lead through a meadow and out to an environmentally sensitive (dogs prohibited) salt flat. A wide, well-developed trail heads south from the meadow, hugging a shallow tidal marsh teeming with birds and a duck-loving canal. The trail continues to the Dunsmuir Community Gardens, 1.1 km (0.7 mile) from the trailhead. Herons are prolific, thanks to an area rookery, and the park is also home to a purple martin colony.

To reach Crescent Beach, head west from the parking lot to the picnic area at Wickson Point and pick up the wide Crescent Beach Dyke Trail. Pass (or venture out on) the Wickson Pier and come to the wide, popular, sandy beach. The water is fairly shallow here, warming to a swimmable temperature in the summer, and the tidal flats are extensive. The trail then reaches Sullivan Point and continues south along the beach. To the east are rows of homes, several old and elegant, attesting to this area's long history as a beach getaway. The views out across Boundary Bay are sweeping, including Orcas Island, Saturna Island, the Olympic Mountains, Vancouver Island, Point Roberts, the Burnaby Metrotown skyline, and a procession of North Shore Mountains. At 1.4 km (0.9 mile) from the parking lot, the trail ends at Maple Street.

Sunsets are sublime at Crescent Beach.

GO FARTHER

When the tide is low, you can continue hiking south on the beach. Otherwise, the immediate shoreline is rocky and hemmed in by an active rail line. If conditions are favorable, cross a small creek and continue on the beach, coming to the Christopherson Steps at 0.3 km (0.2 mile). The steps provide safe passage over the rail line to 24 Avenue. Continue south across sand, gravel, mud, and rocks, reaching a railroad underpass at 2.1 km (1.3 miles). Here, you can take a trail 0.4 km (0.25 mile) up the 1001 Steps to 15a Avenue. This wooden staircase (not exactly 1001 steps, but plenty indeed) ascends a ravine and is a popular cardio workout with locals. If you want to walk more after climbing the steps, continue south on 126a Street for 0.3 km (0.2 mile) to pretty Kwomais Point Park, with its nice little network of trails and excellent viewpoint high on Ocean Park Bluff.

47 Crescent Park

DISTANCE:	About 8 km (5 miles) of trails
ELEVATION GAIN:	Up to 60 m (200 feet)
HIGH POINT:	98 m (320 feet)
DIFFICULTY:	Easy
FITNESS:	Walkers, runners, hikers
FAMILY-FRIENDLY:	Yes
DOG-FRIENDLY:	On leash
AMENITIES:	Washrooms, picnic shelters, sports fields, pickleball courts
CONTACT/MAPS:	City of Surrey Parks and Recreation
BEFORE YOU GO:	Park open dawn to dusk
GPS:	N49.052 W122.864

GETTING THERE

Map to: Crescent Parking Lot 3, Surrey, BC. **Transit:** TransLink buses 350, 352, 360. **Parking:** Park in Lot 3. Alternative trailhead parking lots on 132 Street and 128 Street.

One of two large greenbelts on Surrey's Semiahmoo Peninsula, Crescent Park offers a quiet retreat just a couple of kilometers away from the hustle and bustle of South Surrey's commercial districts. Crescent Park contains 52 ha (128 acres) of mostly mature second-growth forest, a small pond, and a couple of meadows. About 8 km (5 miles) of well-built, interconnecting trails traverse the park.

GET MOVING

Much of Crescent Park is the site of a former logging camp, once located here on a bluff above the Nicomekl River. Loggers transported timber along a busy corridor to the river, where it was boomed and floated to sawmills. Today, the park sports stately, mature conifers. And quiet, leafy neighborhoods abutting the park have replaced the stump yards.

A small section of the park along 132 Street has been developed into sports fields, and soccer and cricket matches are often in play. A new pickleball court was added in 2022. But outside of this area, the park is generally quiet. Trails are not marked, but it's easy to get around—a couple of trails circle the park and several others lead to a small pond at its center.

A couple of small meadows break the forest cover, and the forest floor is fairly open. In autumn, vine maples add gold to the emerald canopy of evergreens, and a handful of rhododendrons brighten the forest near the pond.

From the main parking area, it's a quick 0.3 km (0.2 mile) to the pond. A walk following trails around the periphery of the park is about 3 km (1.9 miles). It's easy to walk 5 km (3.1 miles) within the park without repeating a trail section.

Vine maples add touches of gold to Crescent Park's forest in the fall.

GO FARTHER

Follow a park trail south to 24 Avenue between 129B Street and 130 Street. Then cross 24 Avenue and walk south on a trail for 0.4 km (0.25 mile) to a junction at small Huntington Park. A trail heads south here for 0.4 km (0.25 mile) to 20 Avenue. Head left instead, following a wide trail through a greenbelt of linear parks: Bridlewood, Dogwood, and Chantrell. The trail passes many neighborhood connectors before ending in 2.2 km (1.4 miles) at 140 Street. At Dogwood Park, you can enter the gate and let your pooch wander leash-free on about 2.5 km (1.5 miles) of forested trails.

48 Sunnyside Acres Urban Forest Park

DISTANCE:	About 6 km (3.7 miles) of trails
ELEVATION GAIN:	Up to 45 m (150 feet)
HIGH POINT:	128 m (420 feet)
DIFFICULTY:	Easy
FITNESS:	Walkers, runners, hikers
FAMILY-FRIENDLY:	Yes, and Wally Ross Trail is wheelchair-accessible
DOG-FRIENDLY:	On leash
AMENITIES:	Washrooms at adjacent South Surrey Recreation and Arts Centre
CONTACT/MAPS:	City of Surrey Parks and Recreation
BEFORE YOU GO:	Park open dawn to dusk
GPS:	N49.046 W122.821

GETTING THERE

Map to: Sunnyside Acres Urban Forest Park, Surrey, BC. **Transit.** TransLink bus 360. **Parking:** Park in the lot on the north side of 24 Avenue between 144 Street and 146 Street.

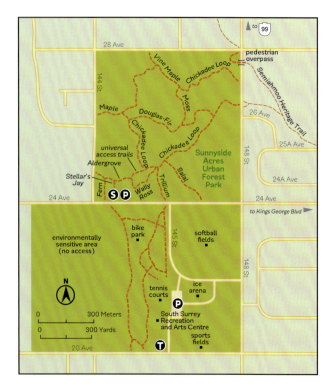

One of the first dedicated urban forest parks in the country, the 140-ha (346-acre) Sunnyside Acres Urban Forest Park protects a large tract of mature forest and excellent wildlife habitat on the Semiahmoo Peninsula. Primarily a natural area, infrastructure is limited to an excellent network of well-maintained trails, including an interpretive nature trail and a universal access trail.

GET MOVING

Logged in the early twentieth century, Sunnyside Acres became a park in 1988 via a vote of the people. Trees in the park are now more than a century old, and many are towering!

And like nearby Crescent Park, the forest understory is graced with vine maples that add beautiful displays of gold in the autumn—many of them arching over the trails. The nonprofit Sunnyside Acres Heritage Society works closely with the Surrey parks department to steward this lovely tract of forest.

The trails are named and signed, allowing for several loop options. The 0.8-km (0.5-mile) Wally Ross Trail loop is a universal access trail, complete with wide boardwalks. The Chickadee Loop is a lovely and popular 2.9-km (1.8-mile) route through a large portion of the forest. It is also an interpretive nature trail with twelve stops along the way. Download the forest's map from the City of Surrey's parks website for the text that corresponds to the stops.

The Trillium and Fern Trails both lead south to cross 24 Avenue (use caution). Here you can follow a near-level trail south for 1 km (0.6 mile) through an impressive stand of conifers to 20 Avenue. Trails also lead to a mountain-bike park and the sports complex at the South Surrey Recreation and Arts Centre. The section of urban forest west of the 24 Avenue–20 Avenue connector trail is closed to public use as an environmentally sensitive area.

This large urban forest supports a healthy population of wildlife, including deer, coyotes, and pileated woodpeckers. Scattered throughout the forest and providing excellent forage material are various berry shrubs, including huckleberry and serviceberry. The latter, commonly referred to as saskatoon in Canada, was the most widely used berry by First Nations residing in the southern half of the province and is still an important food source today.

GO FARTHER

From the northeast end of the forest, you can access the Semiahmoo Heritage Trail. This trail, which is listed on the Canadian Register of Historic Places, follows a section of the historic Semiahmoo Road. This road was built in the 1870s and ran for 40 km (25 miles), connecting New Westminster (at the time the largest city in the Lower Mainland) to Semi-ahmoo in the US (now the city of Blaine, but historically a jumping-off point for prospectors heading north). It was a significant route used by both the area's First Nations and early settlers.

Follow the Semiahmoo Trail south, crossing 148 Street on an overpass. Then continue for 1.8 km (1.1 miles) through a

Chickadee Loop Trail

forested greenbelt and neighborhoods to its southern terminus on 151A Street. You can also follow the trail north by crossing 28 Avenue and then walking along a part of the route that uses a quiet, paved residential road. Pass by Semiahmoo Trail Park with its short network of trails before reaching 32 Avenue. The trail then resumes as single track, reaching its northern terminus in 1.8 km (1.1 miles) at the historic Elgin School on 144 Street. Built in 1921 at the intersection of two important early trade routes, this restored building (also on the Canadian Register of Historic Places) represents the standard school architecture of the time.

49 Elgin Heritage Park

DISTANCE:	5.3 km (3.3 miles) of trails
ELEVATION GAIN:	Minimal
HIGH POINT:	3 m (10 feet)
DIFFICULTY:	Easy
FITNESS:	Walkers, runners, hikers
FAMILY-FRIENDLY:	Yes
DOG-FRIENDLY:	On leash
AMENITIES:	Washrooms, picnic shelters, interpretive signs, Historic Stewart Farm
CONTACT/MAPS:	City of Surrey Parks and Recreation
BEFORE YOU GO:	Park open dawn to dusk
GPS:	N49.066 W122.843

GETTING THERE

Map to: Elgin Heritage Park (Historic Stewart Farm), Surrey, BC. **Transit:** TransLink bus 352; from Nicomekl Greenway's eastern terminus on Elgin Road, it's a short walk to the South Surrey Park and Ride, serviced by TransLink buses 321, 351, 354, 394. **Parking:** Parking is located near the farm and rowing club. Alternative parking at Chantrell Creek parking area 0.25 km (0.4 mile) west on Crescent Road.

Wander through the grounds of a beautifully restored nineteenth-century farm. Hike through meadows and across wildlife-rich marshes. And amble along a dyke on the Nicomekl River—all in this beautiful park that preserves the historical sites and rural landscapes of one of Surrey's earliest settlements.

GET MOVING

Located on the Nicomekl River, Elgin Heritage Park contains a portion of the Stewart Farm, established in 1880 by John Stewart, one of Surrey's first non-Native settlers. This area of early settlement along the navigable river became known as Port Elgin. It thrived as a logging center and later as an important stop on the Semiahmoo Road, which ran from Semiahmoo (now Blaine) in Washington State to New Westminster on the Fraser River. In 1880, Port Elgin was designated as a customs entry point, requiring all travelers to stop and check in. It ceased operations in 1891 after the construction of the Douglas customs point on the international border.

Definitely check out the historic Stewart Farm with its 1894-built Victorian farmhouse, taking time to roam its historical grounds. In spring, enjoy the fragrance and sight of

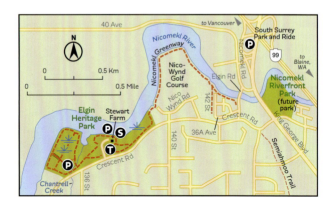

blooming lupines. Throughout the year, a procession of weddings are held at this scenic and lovely spot.

Now hit the trails! From the farm, two trails head west
into forest and converge before crossing Chantrell Creek,
named for the second customs officer at Port Elgin. The trail
then comes to a parking area (alternative trailhead) and a
large meadow. Here three trails branch off, allowing for some
loop options. The trails lead across the meadow, along and
via a boardwalk across a marsh, and along wetlands and the
Nicomekl River. Wildlife viewing, especially bird-watching, is
excellent here. Look for otters, eagles, seals, and owls. Note
the miniature barns built for nesting barn owls.

Nicomekl Greenway Trail along Nicomekl River

From Stewart Farm, two trails also head east into forest. They converge and continue as the Nicomekl Greenway. After paralleling Crescent Road and skirting a large tidal marsh, the trail bends north to meet up with the Nicomekl River. It then follows the river east along a dyke, leaving the park and passing through Nico-Wynd Golf Course. Use caution here and be alert for errant golf balls.

Enjoy good views across the river to productive farmland. One-third of the landmass of this city of 700,000 is dedicated to agriculture. Watch for waterfowl and salmon in the river. Before roads were developed in the area, the Nicomekl River was the main transportation corridor. It takes its name from the Stó:lō First Nation people and means "the route to go," or "the pathway."

Continue along the river, passing interpretive signs about Port Elgin's past and skirting some of the area's newer developments. At 2.1 km (1.3 miles) from the farm, the trail comes to its eastern terminus at Elgin Road. A sign commemorates the historic Semiahmoo Road, replaced here by the Elgin Road.

GO FARTHER

Surrey is currently developing a brand new 32-ha (80-acre) park along 3 km (1.9 miles) of the Nicomekl River just east of Elgin Road. The future Nicomekl Riverfront Park will have several kilometers of riverfront, forest, and meadow trails. The first phase should open in 2025, allowing for an extended hike from the Stewart Farm along the Nicomekl Greenway. Parking and access to the new park will be from King George Boulevard.

South Surrey's Redwood Park (access on 20 Avenue near 180 Street) is also worth a visit. An arboretum founded by two brothers who lived in an on-site treehouse, the park cultivates more than fifty exotic species, including giant sequoias. Wander on 5 km (3.1 miles) of trails in this 32-ha (80-acre) park.

50 Serpentine Fen

DISTANCE:	3.5 km (2.2 miles) roundtrip
ELEVATION GAIN:	Minimal
HIGH POINT:	3 m (10 feet)
DIFFICULTY:	Easy
FITNESS:	Walkers, runners, hikers
FAMILY-FRIENDLY:	Yes
DOG-FRIENDLY:	On leash
AMENITIES:	Viewing towers
CONTACT/MAPS:	Ducks Unlimited; City of Surrey Parks and Recreation
BEFORE YOU GO:	Open dawn to dusk
GPS:	N49.086 W122.815

GETTING THERE

Map to: Serpentine Wildlife Management Area, Surrey, BC.
Transit: TransLink buses 321, 394. **Parking:** Heading north on King George Boulevard, carefully turn left into the trailhead parking area just south of the bridge over the Serpentine River. (Note that the trailhead on 44 Avenue is now closed.)

Hike along the snaking Serpentine River and adjacent marshlands on a series of dykes, built long ago to prevent flooding in the agricultural flats east of Mud Bay. The fen was officially established as the Serpentine Wildlife Management Area (WMA) in 2009. But first, starting in 1975, it was developed by Ducks Unlimited to protect and enhance important habitat for waterfowl and other migratory birds. Like adjacent Mud Bay and Boundary Bay, the 71-ha (175-acre) Serpentine Fen is one of the best places in the Lower Mainland for bird-watching. A trio of observation decks here will enhance your visit.

GET MOVING

From the parking area, head west on a wide trail along a dyke embracing the Serpentine River. Like the nearby Nicomekl

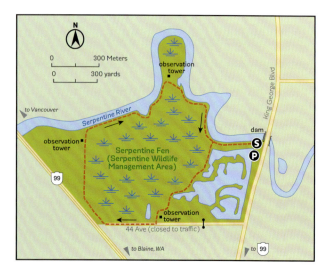

River, this small but ecologically important waterway snakes through a large floodplain that was once composed of marsh and salt flats. The area has since been transformed into a primarily agricultural zone. Near the two rivers' confluence with Mud Bay, the fen is an important stop for birds on the Pacific Flyway migratory route. Look for herons, mallards, wigeons, pintails, green-winged teals, hooded and common mergansers, cormorants, bald eagles, ospreys, red-tailed hawks, northern harriers, and many other species—more than 130 in all.

At 0.3 km (0.2 mile) come to a junction. Head left or right; it's a loop, so you can pick either one. Heading left, the trail skirts a large marshy area and follows along thick hedgerows and through hawthorn tunnels. At 1 km (0.6 mile), it comes to the first observation tower. The trail then heads west on the closed-to-traffic 44 Avenue before bending right, skirting BC 99, and heading across a meadow. Look for rabbits and voles, and perhaps a coyote looking for rabbits and voles. Traffic noise from the freeway may make it hard to hear birdsong here.

At 2 km (1.2 mile), reach the second observation tower, which provides good viewing over wetlands to the east and west. The trail then continues north and intersects the dyke along the Serpentine's southern riverfront. Head right along the river. Aside from waterfowl and wading birds, look for river otters, muskrats, and the occasional harbor seal. Within confined banks, the river level here fluctuates greatly with the tides. Rich, glistening mudflats are revealed during low tide. At 2.7 km (1.7 mile), reach the third observation tower at a sharp oxbow in the river.

Then continue walking along the river, enjoying good views out across the floodplain to the Golden Ears peaks and Mount Baker. At 3.2 km (2 miles), return to the loop junction. Continue straight for 0.3 km (0.2 mile) back to the trailhead.

The trail follows a dyke along the Serpentine River.

WHITE ROCK

51 White Rock Promenade

DISTANCE:	4.4 km (2.7 miles) roundtrip
ELEVATION GAIN:	Minimal
HIGH POINT:	6 m (20 feet)
DIFFICULTY:	Easy
FITNESS:	Walkers, runners
FAMILY-FRIENDLY:	Yes, and wheelchair- and jogging stroller–friendly
DOG-FRIENDLY:	Yes, on 2-m (6-foot) leash; prohibited on promenade April 1–Sept 30 and year-round on pier
AMENITIES:	Washrooms, picnic tables, interpretive signs, benches, museum
CONTACT/MAPS:	City of White Rock Recreation and Culture
BEFORE YOU GO:	Access is from paid parking lots
GPS:	N49.016 W122.790

GETTING THERE

Map to: Ocean Promenade Hotel, White Rock, BC. **Transit:** TransLink buses 361, 362. **Parking:** Park in lots along Marine Drive paralleling the promenade, near Finlay Street.

Stroll, saunter, jog, or take a *passeggiata* along White Rock's promenade, admiring sculptures, historical sites, seabirds, seals, and sweeping views across Semiahmoo Bay to Washington's Semiahmoo Peninsula and Orcas Island. Along with the city pier (the longest in Canada), the promenade is the pride of the "City by the Sea." Locals and tourists from near and far have been enjoying it for more than a century.

GET MOVING

The promenade runs for 2.2 km (1.4 miles)—from East Beach to West Beach—along White Rock's busy commercial district with its restaurants, ice cream parlors, bars, cafés, and shops. You can run or power-walk the promenade out

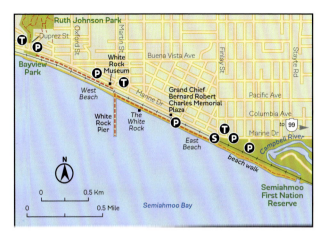

and back in less than an hour. But it's meant to be enjoyed slowly. Savor its sights, smells, and sounds, and delight in all of its charms—sculptures, displays, bird-watching, people-watching, and sunsets.

The brick and paved path parallels a busy rail line. It was this railroad line, connecting Seattle to Vancouver, that stimulated the growth of White Rock (then a ward of Surrey) into a coastal retreat. Owing to its proximity to the international border (pretty much a hop, skip, or paddle away), White Rock flourished during the American Prohibition when visiting Yanks sought out spirits to go along with their leisure. Semiahmoo Bay was also a bootlegger hotbed during the same time period. Enjoy the descriptive panels along the walk.

Begin at the eastern end of the promenade at East Beach. Walk west through the East Beach and come to Grand Chief Bernard Robert Charles (Pa-Kwach-Tun) Memorial Plaza with its totems. The plaza honors a longtime respected leader of the Semiahmoo First Nation, whose traditional lands included White Rock and Crescent Beach in Canada, and Point Roberts, Birch Bay, and Drayton Harbor in Washington State.

Continue walking west, coming to White Rock's namesake, a large glacial erratic that was turned white by seabird guano. Today, the rock is covered in white paint to thwart graffiti attempts. Almost midway, come to White Rock Pier, which juts 470 m (1542 feet) into the bay. Canada's longest pier, it definitely warrants a visit, increasing your walk by 1 km (0.6 mile). From the pier, enjoy views of Washington's Twin Sisters Range and Mount Baker, but keep an eye on hovering gulls and pigeons (remember White Rock's white rock!).

West of the pier, the promenade crosses the tracks and comes to the historical train depot, now a museum. It then travels along the West Beach, terminating at Bayview Park, where a short trail leads down to the beach and along the bluff. Consider a stop for coffee, ice cream, or fish and chips on your return.

White Rock's namesake

GO FARTHER

From the trail's eastern terminus near the bear sculpture, you can hike along the beach on the Semiahmoo First Nation Reserve (respect advisories and/or closures) for 1 km (0.6 mile) to the mouth of the Campbell River. From the trail's western terminus near Bayview Park, walk a block up Duprez Street to Ruth Johnson Park, with its wooded trails, stairways, and excellent views of the city and bay.

LANGLEY

52 Campbell Valley Regional Park

DISTANCE:	33 km (20.5 miles) of trails
ELEVATION GAIN:	Up to 152 m (500 feet)
HIGH POINT:	110 m (360 feet)
DIFFICULTY:	Easy to moderate
FITNESS:	Walkers, runners, hikers, bicyclists
FAMILY-FRIENDLY:	Yes, and several trails wheelchair- and jogger stroller–accessible
DOG-FRIENDLY:	On leash, plus a small off-leash area
AMENITIES:	Washrooms, picnic tables and shelters, interpretive signs, historical structures, Nature House, equestrian center, group camping area
CONTACT/MAPS:	Metro Vancouver Regional Parks
BEFORE YOU GO:	Open 7 AM to various closing times
GPS:	N49.018 W122.656

GETTING THERE

Map to: Campbell Valley Regional Park, Langley, BC. **Transit:** TransLink bus 563 stops at the intersection of 200 Street and 20 Avenue, near the Perimeter trailhead in northwest corner of park. **Parking:** From 8 Avenue, turn left into the South Valley Entrance to access the park and trailhead.

Alternative parking and trailhead can be found at the North Valley Entrance off 16 Avenue.

Langley's largest park, Campbell Valley sprawls for 547 ha (1352 acres), encompassing old pastures, orchards, maturing second-growth forest, small ponds, extensive marshes, and several kilometers of frontage along the Little Campbell River. The park was created from six historical farm plots. Many structures from the Annand/Rowlatt Farmstead still stand and can be visited. The red barn is now the Nature House (open summer weekends), and the farmhouse is still used as a residence, so respect the tenant's privacy there.

Campbell Valley is extremely popular with area equestrians—several trails are shared by pedestrians and horses.

Hikers and walkers should always yield to horseback riders. Campbell Valley also has a long trail shared with cyclists, and several kilometers of trails open to wheelchairs and jogging strollers. The park can get busy, but most activity takes place on the Little River Loop and South Valley Trails. There is plenty of room to roam, and the park's extensive and well-built trail system makes it an excellent place for trail running.

GET MOVING

Consider exploring some of the following trails, and combine them to create loops of varying lengths. From the South Valley Entrance, follow the South Valley Trail for 0.7 km (0.4 mile), descending to the Little River Loop Trail. This trail, the most popular and attractive in the park, makes a 2.3-km (1.4-mile) loop around a bird-rich, marshy stretch of the Little Campbell River. The loop includes two long bridges crossing the river and some boardwalk stretches. The alder and conifer forests lining the way are attractive, with many mature groves. The loop is fairly level and completely wheelchair-accessible (when accessed from the North Valley Entrance).

The wide Perimeter Trail, open to wheelchairs and bikes, begins in the park's extreme northwest corner and traverses forests and meadows along the park's western boundary, reaching the South Valley Entrance in 7.4 km (4.6 miles). You can continue on recently built tread, passing the 1924-built Lochiel Schoolhouse (relocated here from 16 Avenue and 227 Street), which is now used as a museum. Then travel along the southern boundary of the park, wandering through more meadows and passing the access to the off-leash dog area. Continue east to a small loop that departs and reconnects with the trail before reaching its terminus at 2.4 km (1.5 miles), by the Shaggy Mane Trail and a bridge crossing the Little Campbell River.

Little Campbell River

The 1.8-km (1.1-mile) Ravine Trail loop begins from the Annand/Rowlatt Farmstead. One of the first farms in the Campbell Valley, it was cleared in 1886 by pioneer Alexander Annand from Nova Scotia. The trail follows a stretch of an old logging railroad grade before reaching the river and climbing back up to the farm grounds.

For a grand hike or run around the park, take to the Shaggy Mane Trail. As its name suggests, this is a horse-friendly trail. Follow it north from the South Valley Entrance past the Carvolth Ponds. The way heads east past an open riding area before passing through the North Valley Entrance and crossing the river. It then bends south, climbing a small hill before reaching the Campbell Downs Equestrian Centre (access from 208 Street). The trail then travels southeast, passing an old access road to the historic Langley Speedway, which operated from 1965 until 1984 and once hosted NASCAR races (one of only three places in British Columbia to do so). Check it out, or keep following Shaggy Mane to the Little Campbell River.

The trail crosses the river and then heads west across old pastures. Then it bends north, passing the Lochiel Schoolhouse and returning to the South Valley Entrance. The entire loop is 11 km (6.8 miles). Along the way, the Shaggy Mane Trail connects to many of the park's other trails, offering lots of loop options for longer hikes or runs.

GO FARTHER

A short distance east of Campbell Valley Regional Park is the Municipal Natural Park on 224 Street. Here, you can walk on a lightly traveled trail for 1.7 km (1.1 miles) through forest and along fields, crossing the Little Campbell River twice before reaching 232 Street.

53 Derby Reach Regional Park

DISTANCE:	13 km (8.1 miles) of trails
ELEVATION GAIN:	Up to 61 m (200 feet)
HIGH POINT:	46 m (150 feet)
DIFFICULTY:	Easy
FITNESS:	Walkers, runners, hikers, bicyclists
FAMILY-FRIENDLY:	Yes, and some trails wheelchair- and jogger stroller–accessible
DOG-FRIENDLY:	Both on-leash and off-leash areas
AMENITIES:	Washrooms, picnic tables, campground, interpretive signs, historical buildings and sites, equestrian trails
CONTACT/MAPS:	Metro Vancouver Regional Parks
BEFORE YOU GO:	Open 7 AM to various closing times
GPS:	N49.208 W122.617

GETTING THERE

Map to: Edgewater Bar Campground, Langley Township, BC. **Transit:** TransLink bus 562 stops in Fort Langley at the corner of Glover Road and 96 Avenue, requiring a 0.4-km

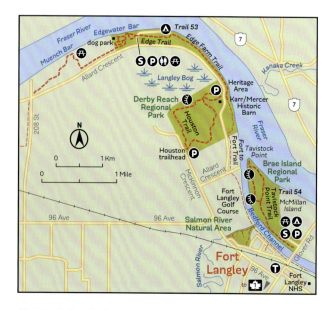

(0.25-mile) walk via Glover Road to the Fort to Fort trailhead.
Parking: Park at the Edgewater Bar trailhead in Derby Reach.
Alternative parking and trailhead at Heritage Area, 2.1 km (1.3
miles) east on Allard Crescent, and Houston trailhead on
McKinnon Crescent.

Hike or run along the Fraser River, skirting farms, traversing groves of towering cottonwoods, and taking in views of
the majestic Golden Ears peaks along the way. Head into a
mature forest of cedars, firs, and hemlocks at the edge of
a sprawling bog, home to myriad wildlife, including sandhill
cranes. And check out the original location of Fort Langley,
which led to the creation of British Columbia.

GET MOVING

Edgewater Bar can be a busy place. Families and friends often
congregate at picnic shelters and fire pits. And folks are

usually fishing or wading in the Fraser River. The Trans Canada/Canyon to Coast Trail passes through here, and that's what you want to check out.

You can follow the trail west, crossing a creek and coming to the park's large and popular off-leash area. Skirt the fenced dog park and pass through a former pasture, complete with metal cow silhouettes. At 0.6 km (0.4 mile), the trail parallels Allard Crescent, passing an active farm. Enter the park's lightly visited Muench Bar unit (the former homestead of one of Langley's founders) at 1.3 km (0.8 mile). After passing a spur to a picnic area on the river, follow the trail through meadows and forest, reaching 208 Street and the park's end at 2.9 km (1.8 miles). The trail continues beyond, paralleling roadways.

An overlook of Langley Bog

Derby Reach's more interesting features lie east of Edgewater Bar (be sure to pick up an interpretive pamphlet at the trailhead kiosk). Follow the Edge Trail (part of the Trans Canada/Canyon to Coast Trail) east, skirting the park's campground through an impressive grove of towering cottonwoods. The trail then reaches the end of the campground road before resuming as the Edge Farm Trail. Continue through meadows and forest along the Fraser River, with impressive views of the waterway, logging booms, and the Golden Ears hovering over the city of Maple Ridge.

At 2.6 km (1.6 miles) from the trailhead, come to the park's Heritage Area, the site of the original Fort Langley. From 1827 to 1839, Fort Langley (the first European settlement in coastal British Columbia) occupied this bluff on

FORT LANGLEY: THE BIRTHPLACE OF BRITISH COLUMBIA

Today the village of Fort Langley on the Fraser River in Langley Township is a quaint community with several riverside parks. It's also the home of Parks Canada's Fort Langley National Historic Site, where the colony of British Columbia was first proclaimed.

In 1824, the Hudson Bay Company (HBC) established Fort Vancouver on the Columbia River in what is now Washington State as its fur trade headquarters for the Rocky Mountains and Pacific Coast regions. The latter—referred to as Columbia District by the British and as Oregon Country by the Americans—was part of a territorial dispute between the two nations. Fearing that Fort Vancouver would be lost to the Americans if the Columbia River didn't become the international border, Sir George Simpson (governor of the HBC) called for the construction of Fort Langley on the Fraser River in 1827.

The fort was first constructed in what is now Derby Reach Regional Park. In 1839, the fort was moved upriver 4 km (2.5 miles) to where the NHS is presently situated. Its focus changed from fur trading to farming, fishing, and cranberry harvesting. Fort Langley was a diverse place, with HBC workers of Scottish, French, Kanaka (Hawaiian), Métis, Iroquois, and Cree descent. Area First Nations traded at the fort.

Derby Reach (see sidebar). Check out the interpretive displays. The trail continues east as the Fort to Fort Trail (see Go Farther below). Across the road from the original fort site is the 1909-built Houston House (a private residence), the 1876-built Karr/Mercer Historic Barn, and the Houston Trail.

The Houston Trail makes a lovely 4-km (2.5-mile) loop (with a couple of short, steep sections) through a lush forest of mature cedars, Sitka spruce, maples, and firs and skirts the ecologically important Langley Bog. Look for sundews (a carnivorous plant) and nesting sandhill cranes. An observation deck offers excellent views of this threatened ecosystem. The Langley Bog once covered more than 485 ha (1200 acres), but 90 percent of it has since been mined for peat or converted into cranberry fields.

HBC encouraged its workers to marry Indigenous women to strengthen alliances, and Indigenous workers were employed at the fort's farm. Chinook Jargon was widely used for communicating.

Fort Langley grew dramatically during the 1858 Fraser Canyon Gold Rush, acting as a staging point for prospectors. Thirty thousand people, mostly Americans, descended upon the region, leading the British Parliament to hastily establish a crown colony on the Pacific mainland. On November 19, 1858, James Douglas (HBC chief factor and governor of the colony of Vancouver Island) announced the establishment of the colony of British Columbia from Fort Langley. It was a preemptive move to thwart the United States from annexing the district. But Fort Langley's role as provisional capital of the new colony was short-lived. In February 1859, Colonel Moody ordered the construction of a new capital at New Westminster, as its position was more defensible.

In 1866, the colonies of Vancouver Island and British Columbia were joined, with Victoria as its capital. In 1871, British Columbia entered Confederation, becoming Canada's sixth province. Fort Langley went into decline, closing as a company post in 1886. In 1923, Canada designated Fort Langley as a National Historic Site. Only one original building, the storehouse, remains. However, many buildings were reconstructed, and the site is now a lively reproduction of the historical fort, with interpretive and educational displays, programs, and events.

GO FARTHER

Follow the Fort to Fort Trail south through rolling meadows granting excellent views of the Golden Ears and Mount Baker hovering over the Fraser River. The trail then skirts the Allard Crescent for 0.6 km (0.4 mile) before heading into forest and then hugging the Fraser River shoreline, reaching the village of Fort Langley in 3.8 km (2.4 miles). En route, pass interpretive signs and good views of Brae Island (see Trail 54) across Bedford Channel. At Fort Langley, wander short trails along the Salmon River, to the Heritage CNR (Canadian National Railway) Station, and at Marina Park. Walk 0.5 km (0.3 mile) up Mavis Avenue to reach the Fort Langley National Historic Site. And plan on getting lunch or a coffee in the delightful village.

54 | Brae Island Regional Park

DISTANCE:	4.8-km (3-mile) loop
ELEVATION GAIN:	Minimal
HIGH POINT:	18 m (60 feet)
DIFFICULTY:	Easy
FITNESS:	Walkers, runners, hikers, bicyclists
FAMILY-FRIENDLY:	Yes, and wheelchair- and jogger stroller–accessible
DOG-FRIENDLY:	On leash
AMENITIES:	Washrooms, picnic tables, campground
CONTACT/MAPS:	Metro Vancouver Regional Parks
BEFORE YOU GO:	Open 7 AM to various closing times
GPS:	N49.173 W122.575

GETTING THERE

Map to: Brae Island Regional Park, Langley, BC. **Transit:** TransLink bus 562 stops in Fort Langley at the corner of Glover Road and 96 Avenue, requiring a 0.8-km (0.5-mile)

The author and his son enjoy the view from Tavistock Point.

walk via Glover Road to trailhead. **Parking:** After crossing onto McMillan Island, turn left into Brae Island Regional Park and then immediately left to reach the trailhead and parking.

Explore an island on the Fraser River near historic Fort Langley, the birthplace of British Columbia. Wander through towering cottonwoods and explore beaches and mudflats along the river. Enjoy excellent views, too, of BC's longest river, the prominent Golden Ears, North Shore peaks, and other Coast Range mountains.

GET MOVING

Brae Island was once separated from McMillan Island by a narrow channel, but the construction of the Jacob Haldi Bridge in the 1920s caused sedimentation to fill the west end of the channel, creating one island. Brae Island, no longer much of an island, now mostly consists of the 69-ha (170-acre) Brae Island Regional Park. McMillan Island is the reserve land of the Kwantlen First Nation and home to their band office. Prior to European settlement and colonization, the Kwantlen (a Stó:lō people) were one of the most populous First Nations in the Lower Mainland. They were instrumental in the fur trade operations at Hudson's Bay Company's (HBC) Fort Langley.

From the day-use parking area, follow the Tavistock Point Trail, skirting the park's Fort Camping area and traveling along Bedford Channel. Pass a canoe-launching area and picnic grounds. The trail traverses a forest of alders and cottonwoods with a thick understory. Water can pool on the forest floor in spring, resulting in summer visits by swarms of mosquitoes.

At 1.1 km (0.7 mile), the trail splits, offering you a loop option. The trail to the left passes two short spurs to viewpoints along the channel, meeting up with the trail departing right in 0.8 km (0.5 mile). The trail leading right reaches the Fraser River and then travels along it. Look out at log booms on the wide river. Before the Golden Ears Bridge was built in 2009, you could watch the Albion Ferry crossing the river from McMillan Island. This trail branch reconnects with the channel side in 1.1 km (0.7 mile).

From the junction where the two trail branches reconnect, continue 0.3 km (0.2 mile) north to Tavistock Point. Take a break on the bench and enjoy the view downriver. Or, if tidal conditions permit, explore the small sandy and muddy beach at the point. The Fraser River is tidal all the way to the city of Mission, more than 130 km (80 miles) from its mouth on the Strait of Georgia.

GO FARTHER

Combine your trip with a visit to Fort Langley National Historic Site (see sidebar). Or hike or run on the Fort to Fort Trail through the Salmon River Natural Area to Derby Reach Regional Park (Trail 53).

55 Aldergrove Regional Park

DISTANCE:	More than 15 km (9 miles) of trails
ELEVATION GAIN:	Up to 152 m (500 feet)
HIGH POINT:	90 m (300 feet)
DIFFICULTY:	Easy
FITNESS:	Walkers, runners, hikers, bicyclists
FAMILY-FRIENDLY:	Yes, and several trails wheelchair- and jogger stroller–accessible
DOG-FRIENDLY:	On leash, plus small off-leash area
AMENITIES:	Washrooms, picnic tables and shelters, interpretive signs, historical structures, equestrian trails
CONTACT/MAPS:	Metro Vancouver Regional Parks
BEFORE YOU GO:	Open 7 AM to various closing times
GPS:	N49.0119 W122.465

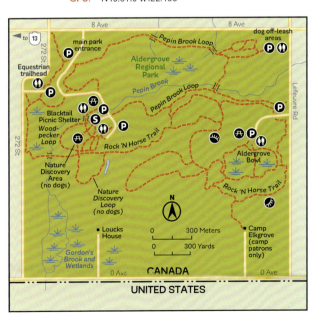

GETTING THERE

Map to: Aldergrove Regional Park, Langley, BC. **Parking:** Park at the main day-use area and trailhead near the Blacktail Picnic Shelter. Alternative parking and trailhead at Aldergrove Bowl off Lefeuvre Road

Sitting on the 49th parallel, Aldergrove Regional Park offers spectacular views of the agriculturally rich Nooksack Valley surrounding Lynden and the glacier-clad volcano Mount Baker (both in Washington State). The eastern section of this park was once a large gravel quarry, but it has since been restored to a natural state. The remainder of the park is graced with mature second-growth forest; grassy, wildlife-rich marshlands; and riparian habitats along Pepin Brook supporting several at-risk species—including the Nooksack dace, Pacific water shrew, and Salish sucker.

GET MOVING

Straddling the Langley-Abbottsford line, this park is fully managed by the MVRD Parks Department, even though Abbottsford lies within the Fraser Valley Regional District. Management and land-use changes have long been part of Aldergrove's history. Starting as a private beach at the now-defunct Aldergrove Lake, the park has grown to 259 ha (640 acres), complete with a wonderful trail system.

From the main day-use area, children will want to check out the short trails in the Nature Discovery Area (dogs prohibited), which includes a climbing stump, sand play area, stepping stones, and other features that encourage bonding with nature through play. The delightful hiker-only 0.5-km (0.3-mile) Nature Discovery Loop (dogs prohibited) travels through a lush, saturated meadow in the Pepin Brook floodplain. But don't follow an unofficial trail through sensitive habitat to the historic, 1909-built Loucks House. If you want to view the house, see it from 0 Avenue.

You can also take the family for a hike on the delightful 3.5-km (2.2-mile) Pepin Brook Loop. Heading east, the trail travels along the brook's floodplain and across a large marsh on a long bridge and boardwalk. It then heads west, climbing and rolling through forested uplands and crossing a couple of cascading creeks. At a small meadow, it begins its descent back to the park's main day-use area.

The international border sports good views of Mount Baker and farmland.

A short trail from the main day-use area leads south to connect with the wide, 6-km (3.7-mile) Rock 'N Horse Trail, which is multiuse. This trail starts at the park's northwestern corner and passes through the Equestrian trailhead before descending to cross Pepin Brook. It then heads east through mature timber, ascending to the Aldergrove Bowl, an active quarry until the 1960s. It was later converted into a pond popular for swimming, but it was drained in 2011 due to health and other issues. It was eventually replanted with native vegetation. A small wetland was also created within the bowl. The Rock 'N Horse Trail loops around the bowl, passing by a humongous glacial erratic before climbing its grassy, open rim. Views are superb of Mount Baker, the Cheam Range, and other North Cascades peaks. Enjoy excellent views, too, of the broad Nooksack floodplain and its grid of farms, spread out south of the 49th parallel.

You can extend your wandering by following a series of short trails around the wetlands in the bowl. And a 1.5-km (0.9-mile), hiker-only trail loops around the broad, open hillside west of the bowl.

GO FARTHER

Kitty-corner to the park's northwest corner is Jackman Wetlands Park and Raptors Knoll Disc Golf Park. The latter has been ranked by UDisc as one of the world's best courses. It was built on old industrial land, since reclaimed by native vegetation. The adjacent wetlands are reclaimed gravel quarries. Birding is excellent at the wetlands, and there are good views of North Shore peaks and Mount Baker from the knoll. A trail system of about 4 km (2.5 miles) traverses the two areas. You can hike here from Aldergrove by carefully crossing 8 Avenue where the Rock 'N Horse Trail begins, or you can park at a trailhead off 272 Street. Be mindful of flying discs while walking through the disc golf park!

RESOURCES

TRAIL AND PARK MANAGEMENT

Bowen Island Municipality
https://bowentrails.ca/about

British Columbia Provincial Parks
https://bcparks.ca/find-a-park

City of Burnaby Parks, Recreation and Culture
www.burnaby.ca/explore-outdoors/parks

City of New Westminster Parks and Recreation
www.newwestcity.ca/parks-and-recreation/parks/community-parks

City of Richmond Parks and Recreation
www.richmond.ca/parks-recreation/parks

City of Surrey Parks and Recreation
www.surrey.ca/parks-recreation/parks

City of Vancouver Department of Streets and Transportation
https://vancouver.ca/streets-transportation/explore-the-arbutus-greenway.aspx

City of Vancouver Parks, Recreation and Cultural Services
www.cityofvancouver.us/community/parks-trails/parkfinder

City of White Rock Recreation and Culture
www.whiterockcity.ca/401/Pier-Promenade

Coquitlam Parks, Recreation, Culture and Facilities
www.coquitlam.ca/Facilities/Facility/Details/Mundy-Park-59

District of North Vancouver Parks, Trails & Recreation
https://dnv.org/parks-trails-recreation

District of West Vancouver Parks and Recreation
https://westvancouver.ca/parks-recreation/parks-trails

George C. Reifel Migratory Bird Sanctuary
www.reifelbirdsanctuary.com

Lynn Canyon Park and Ecology Centre
https://ecologycentre.ca

Metro Vancouver Regional Parks
https://metrovancouver.org/services/regional-parks/find-a-regional-park

Whatcom County Parks and Recreation
https://www.whatcomcounty.us/1913/Parks-Trails

TRAIL, RECREATION, AND CONSERVATION ORGANIZATIONS

BC Mountaineering Club (BCMC)
www.bcmc.ca

BC Parks Foundation
https://bcparksfoundation.ca

Bowen Island Trail Society
https://bowenislandtrailsociety.ca

Burnaby Lake Park Association
https://burnabylakepark.ca/who-we-are

Burns Bog Conservation Society
https://burnsbog.org

Colony Farm Park Association
https://colonyfarmpa.com

Ducks Unlimited Canada
www.ducks.ca

Fraser Valley Conservancy
https://fraservalleyconservancy.ca

Friends of Cypress Provincial Park
https://cypresspark.ca

Golden Age Hiking Club
https://gahc.ca

Green Timbers Heritage Society
www.greentimbers.ca

Lighthouse Park Preservation Society
www.lpps.ca

Lions Gate Road Runners
https://lgrr.com

Little Campbell Watershed Society
www.littlecampbellriver.org

Metro Vancouver Regional Parks Foundation
https://mvrpfoundation.ca

Minnekhada Park Association
www.minnekhada.ca

Nature Vancouver
https://naturevancouver.ca

North Shore Hikers
https://northshorehikers.org

Pacific Spirit Park Society
http://pacificspiritparksociety.org/about-the-park/pacific-spirit-park

Richmond Nature Park Society
www.richmondnatureparksociety.ca

Sunnyside Acres Heritage Society
www.sunnysideacres.ca

Vancouver Botanical Gardens Association
www.vandusengarden.org

Whatcom Parks and Recreation Foundation
www.wprfoundation.org

Wreck Beach Preservation Society
www.wreckbeach.org

ACKNOWLEDGMENTS

AS WITH ALL OF MY previous books, researching and writing *Urban Trails: Vancouver, BC* was fun, gratifying, and a lot of hard work. I have long wanted to write this book, and when the Covid-19 pandemic shut down the border it forced me to wait a little longer to do it. But it was incredibly satisfying to spend so much time in the Metro Vancouver Regional District. Vancouver is truly one of my favorite cities in the world.

I couldn't have finished this project without the help and support of the following people. A huge thank you to all the great people at Mountaineers Books, especially publisher, Tom Helleberg; editor in chief, Kate Rogers; and project editor, Susan Elderkin.

A big thank you to my editor, Emily Estes, for her attention to detail and thoughtful suggestions, helping to make this book a finer volume. It was a pleasure working with her during what is one of the hardest processes for me in putting a book together! I also want to thank my wife, Heather, and my son, Giovanni, for accompanying me on many of the trails in this book—and to all the great Asian restaurants afterward! A big thanks, too, to Judith Romano, Richard Romano, Suzanne Gerber, and Stephen Hui for providing me with excellent trail company. And I thank God for watching over me and keeping me safe and healthy while I hiked and ran all over the MVRD!

INDEX

ABOUT THE AUTHOR

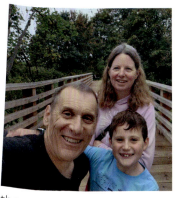

Craig Romano grew up in rural New Hampshire, where he fell in love with the natural world. He moved to Washington in 1989 and has since hiked more than 35,000 miles in Washington and British Columbia alone. An avid runner as well, Craig has run more than one hundred half marathons, and forty marathons and ultra runs, including the Boston Marathon and the Cuyamaca 100K Endurance Run.

Craig is the award-winning author of more than twenty-five books. His *Columbia Highlands: Exploring Washington's Last Frontier* was recognized in 2010 by Washington Secretary of State Sam Reed and State Librarian Jan Walsh as a "Washington Reads" book for its contribution to Washington's cultural heritage. Craig also writes for numerous publications, tourism websites, and Hikeoftheweek.com, and provides content for the TREAD Map app.

Craig lives with his wife, son, and cat in Skagit County, Washington, less than 80 km (50 miles) from the Canadian border, allowing him to run and hike frequently in the Greater Vancouver area. Visit him online at CraigRomano.com, on Facebook at "Craig Romano Guidebook Author," and on Instagram at craig.romano.

Craig Romano, with his wife, Heather, and son, Giovanni.

YOU MAY ALSO LIKE:

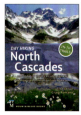
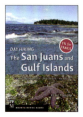

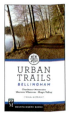